ENDORSEMENTS

The challenge as physicians comes when we are confronted with the patient diagnosed with a terminal or life-altering illness and a straight forward "cure" is unavailable. With this book, a doctor's tool box will never again be empty, even when there is nothing medically left to do.

—*Joy Twillie, M.D.*
PSYCHIATRIST, TN

Jim, having passed through the loss of a loved one, has put together a "how to" manual for others who face the possibility of loss. Here are the step by step guidelines which can walk a person through the ominous clouds which gather at the impending loss of a loved one. Because this subject is so sensitive, only someone who has passed through it has the compassionate insights to lead the way for others to see the sun beyond the clouds.

This book should be in the hands of every counselor, for at some time in every life this situation will arise and *After Diagnosis: Life* will be the prescription needed to give hope in what seems to be the darkest night.

—*Rev. Paul Johansson*
CHANCELLOR EMERITUS,
ELIM BIBLE INSTITUTE

To anyone who has worked with terminally ill patients, it is very clear that these patients easily figure out who really cares for them and who doesn't. Even physicians at times "flee" . . . Jim stands by what he practices and teaches, and those he ministers to know it.

—*Matthew Y. Suh, MD, MPH*
LIVER AND PANCREAS SURGEON, NJ

Tomorrow, three days, three weeks, three years—whatever time you have left on this earth—God wants you to enjoy a full and abundant life. Jim Henry's book *After Diagnosis: LIFE* inspires you to make the each moment your best moment.

—*Pat Gano*
No. Manchester, IN

Through Jim and The Life Givers Network I've been empowered to live intentionally, facing my fears, changing my perspective, getting new vision for both myself and my group. I've come to realize there are treasures to be found in the darkness that we are sometimes called to walk through. I am always discovering more about God, about my walk with Him, and gaining new wisdom to provide others with a safe place to voice their thoughts and feelings when encountering life challenges.

—*Diane Mueller*
New Jersey - Caregiver and Group Leader

The book you are about to read is revolutionary . . . simple, and so straightforward. It reveals how to change your process from dying to living. This book provides the reader with a simple and yet complete statement of what is needed no matter if it is ten seconds or ten years since you heard the diagnosis that rocked your world. Jim has captured the very essence of hope in this new book.

—*Dr. David Wesner*
Pastor, Faith Outreach, Clarksville, TN

My experiences with Jim Henry and The Life Givers Network have consistently underscored Jim's passion and understanding for those walking through a life-threatening crisis. This work reaches people facing great challenges and offers hope, healing, and the choice to live life to the fullest, making it a true gift from God.

—Rev. Rich Higby
PASTORAL CARE, CORNERSTONE
CHRISTIAN CHURCH, WYCKOFF, NJ

. . . a life-changing book that effectively shows how to live life in spite of severe circumstances.

—Gail Singer
NEW JERSEY, CANCER SURVIVOR
AND LIFE GIVER GROUP LEADER

After Diagnosis: Life is a breath of fresh air tackling an area that for too long has been viewed as doom and gloom! Jim writes with a passion that jumps off the page and into the heart of the reader . . . it's a must read . . . its words speak of the hope that gives life not death.

—Joe Pellegrino
FOUNDER & PRESIDENT, LEGACY MINDED MEN

The experience of three heart attacks, a stroke, and five heart operations has shown me that the Lord is truly in control. I believe Life Givers is an important part of the Lords promise to give his people the very best that this life can offer. To be able to put doubt to one side and to live is so wonderful only the Lord can make this possible, thank you Jim from all the people that can benefit from this wonderful book.

—Mike Starbuck
LEICESTER, UK

The substance of this book is how to live not how to die. It takes people beyond hopelessness and despair . . . reminding those who are terminally ill that they can be useful to Christ and for His Kingdom . . . through the indomitable spirit which is purified by the Holy Spirit who enables us, empowers us, sanctifies us, adopts us, provides us with grace in abundance, and makes us witnesses for Christ and His church. Thank you for putting skin, heart, soul, and substance on an often misunderstood subject.

—*Dr. Peter Padro*
INNER CITY MISSIONARY WITH
WORLD IMPACT, RETIRED, PA

After our lives were turned upside down because I had intestinal surgery and was in and out of the ER for more than a year. My wife noticed a lump on her neck which turned out to be Stage 5 lymphoma. We were shocked and overwhelmed. What we have learned through Life Givers has given us a better hold on God's love and protective hand. We've learned to say "what's next" instead of saying 'why me' and we live each day with a smile that has been making life complete.

—*Tony & Frannie Lombardi*
SURVIVORS AND FRIENDS OF LIFE GIVERS

ADDITIONAL COMMENTS ABOUT
AFTER DIAGNOSIS: LIFE

". . . it's simple, straightforward, and easy to apply" —*NJ*

"It's outstanding . . ." —*NJ*

"Easy to read . . . guides people in crisis towards Christ-centered living" —*FL*

"It helped me have a better understanding of the challenges terminally ill people face" —*FL*

"It's a message whose time has come" —*MI*

"Jim's work helps people live in the natural realm and bridge the gap between what God is doing in the supernatural and what hope there is in the natural" —*Dr. in TN*

"Emphasizing the love God has for His children . . . the peace and life He offers . . . this book will challenge you to redirect your focus and restructure your thinking" —*Korea*

"This sincere, simple book has enriched our walk with God and our lives immensely" —*TN*

"The legacy we can leave our children is hope . . . not grief . . . they are watching me and I will show them that life after devastation will and must go on . . . Show our children we can and will survive and so will they . . ." —*RI*

"Working for hospice and in hospitals I've encountered many people with life threatening diseases . . . after reading Jim's book I wished it had been available years earlier . . . mainly to let them know there is life after being diagnosed and how to fight to live . . ." —*TN*

"It is giving me lots of hope and direction for the days ahead"—*a new widow, MI*

"This is the dawn of a new day for me . . . your book is mentoring me in it . . ."

"I left the seminar strengthened in heart and spirit with a clear sense that God does see, love, and care about us when we think we have been abandoned . . ." —*NJ*

"I can truly say that Life Givers saved my life and allowed me to find my purpose" —*NJ*

"I particularly liked this idea in your book: 'After 38 years of trouble and blessing . . . I can honestly say "I know that I know." And what I know is that God is real and the only one we can count on.'" —*NJ*

". . . the book is compelling; I couldn't put it down. It's understandable, well-written, and empowering." —*MA*

"Your book has been so helpful in realizing my purpose . . ." —*NJ*

"It truly provides life-saving HOPE . . . without HOPE we have nothing . . . with HOPE we not only survive, but can overcome every obstacle . . ." —*NJ*

"This book is an aid to help you take a stand, then a step to turn your life around . . . to live stronger, wiser, and more whole than ever before." —*NJ*

". . . is a must read for anyone who has just been diagnosed with a life-threatening illness and for their care giver." —*NJ*

"It explains step-by-step, with great compassion and wisdom, how you can fully LIVE regardless of your situation . . ." —*NJ*

"Your book was the catalyst to start praying how the Lord wants to use me now."

"I began to journal as I read: write the vision so you can run. Life is pointing people to Jesus. Life is hope. Life is healing. Life is being blessed to bless others. Life is finding my purpose." —*FL*

"Your book made me want to begin living again . . ." —*SC*

"It's a way of life . . . a message that transforms . . ." —*NJ*

"Your work is not just inspiring or motivational, it's transformational." —*NJ*

". . . wonderful . . . enlightening . . . really helped me understand and put some of my own family experiences into perspective . . ." —*a long-time friend and neighbor*

". . . a very accurate description of the journey that we all shared together . . ." —*a long-time friend and neighbor*

"... with its personal touches at every corner and helpful tools for managing life's most challenging ordeals ... this book helps the reader find answers and always know where to turn and look when they think they have run out of answers." —*a very close family friend*

"You could not have known, but you delivered that book at a moment when some direction and some answers were very much needed ..." —*a neighbor*

AFTER DIAGNOSIS:
LIFE

AFTER DIAGNOSIS:
LIFE

Conquer Your Fear,
Develop Your Life Plan,
Impact Generations To Come

DR. JIM HENRY

Foreword by Kary Oberbrunner
Author of *Your Secret Name* and *The Deeper Path*

DEDICATION

This 20th Anniversary edition is dedicated to Kary Oberbrunner, David Branderhorst, and my fellow Fire Ring Members who will celebrate with me in Columbus, Ohio at The Igniting Souls Conference 2019.

You've challenged and encouraged me to do many things I've never done before. The result is the growing impact, influence, and income that allows me to see my dream of touching untold numbers of lives come alive, day by day.

I would not have kept going if it were not for you. I'm forever grateful for what comes out of this experience as will be the individuals whose lives are transformed.

Jim Henry
Crystal Springs
October 2019

ORIGINAL DEDICATION:

Pastor Victor Coetzee
. . . who for 30 years has been a model of how a shepherd should care for his flock.

Christian Larson
. . . who for the 14 years we knew one another taught me about love and forgiveness after he lost his wife, a daughter, and his eyesight.

Dr. Lawrence LeShan
. . . who was my mentor for over six years as I began working with those critically ill, teaching me about the impact of bringing life to those facing death.

Dr. Craig Ellison
. . . who, though experiencing pain on a daily basis, persisted until his dream came to pass, and then invited me to share my dream from his platform.

Only those who see the invisible can do the impossible.

Dr. B. Lown

CONTENTS

FOREWORD   XIX

ACKNOWLEDGMENTS   XXI

INTRODUCTION   XXV

CHAPTER ONE: BEGINNING   1

CHAPTER TWO: RESPONSE OR REACTION   10

CHAPTER THREE: SEEKING GOD FIRST   20

CHAPTER FOUR: WHAT'S REALLY IMPORTANT?   31

CHAPTER FIVE: PLANNING   42

CHAPTER SIX: DECISION TIME   53

CHAPTER SEVEN: ACT   63

CHAPTER EIGHT: OUTCOMES   75

CHAPTER NINE: WHAT'S NEXT?   85

CHAPTER TEN: MOUNTAINS   91

SUGGESTED READING   95

CONTACT INFORMATION   99

FOREWORD

Jim Henry is a man with a most unusual and remarkable calling. His life radically changed in 1972 when confronted by a friend's 5-year-old son who was dying of cancer. Since then, members of Jim's family received a cancer diagnosis eighteen times. The result is a deep understanding of the shock, panic, despair, and fear one experiences when receiving a dire diagnosis.

Yet, Jim is one who loves life and loves helping those who have been told their life might be ending much sooner than they ever imagined. There's something about Jim that brings calm to a stressful situation. Maybe it's his deep compassion or empathy. However, I believe it is his remarkable faith in a miracle-working God that's been tested time and again. He wants to help you transform your journey, change the expected outcome of your situation, and learn to leave a positive legacy rather than years of grief and sorrow.

Time is of the essence, and Jim can help you cut to the chase, shorten your learning curve, and begin experiencing an abundant life. He knows from personal experience how to transform what could become a tragedy into triumph. Therefore, he can help you redeem the most precious moments of your life if you will allow it.

Kary Oberbrunner, author of
Your Secret Name and *The Deeper Path*

ACKNOWLEDGMENTS

This book would not be possible without the support, encouragement, and cooperation of many people over a very long time. I wish to thank the following:

First, thanks to the countless numbers of patients and their relatives who have allowed me access to the most intimate parts of their lives during challenging days.

All the supporters of James Henry Counseling Associates and The Life Givers Network®, four family foundations in particular, and several corporate partners who made it possible for me to continue living and serving in this area.

Dr. Lawrence LeShan, who agreed to mentor me when I first attempted to care for critically ill people, and who helped me understand I could make a difference in this arena.

Dr. Daniel Moriarty, who opened the door, which allowed me the privilege of working with his patients at

Medical Diagnostics, and let me see the care of critically ill patients through the eyes of a physician.

Diane Mueller, facilitator of the longest-running Life Giver group and caregiver extraordinaire. She helped this work in many ways and supported me as I sought to understand "the heart" of patients and caregivers alike.

Gail Singer, cancer survivor, and Life Giver facilitator, who continually reminds me by how she lives of the potential for patients even while they are going through it.

Pastor Don James and Bethany Church, Wyckoff, NJ, for their long-time support of this work and for hosting the first Life Giver group.

Pastor Frank Bolella and Living Word Community Church, for hosting and supporting the longest-running Life Giver Network group.

Pastors Dave Gustavsen and Paul Rittinger, along with the folks of Jacksonville Chapel, Lincoln Park, NJ, for their support of this work and for hosting one of our longest-running Life Giver groups.

Paul Johansson of Hampton, VA, David Wesner, and Rich Higby for walking with me through difficult life challenges and encouraging me about the potential of my ministry and The Life Givers Network®.

Dr. Ronald Westrate, for his continual encouragement, to understand, develop, and encouragement to use my unique gifts to the fullest extent possible.

Dr. Jimmy Lee of "Living Free" for his encouragement from the days of "Seeds of Light" as well as the beginning days of The Life Givers Network®.

Kevin Miller, Dan Miller, and Chuck Bowen, three men who since 2008 have helped me believe I could do things I never thought possible.

Lee Troup, for his encouragement, guidance, and work with me on this text as I learned the writing process.

David Danglis of Pinwheel Creative in Lima, NY, for his patience with me and help with the cover design and preparation of the manuscript.

My friend Joe Pellegrino, the board and leadership team, and the men of Legacy Minded Men who continue to encourage me daily.

My board that oversees the work of James Henry Counseling Associates and The Life Givers Network®.

Leslie A.H. Sheen, my oldest daughter, who helped her dad with some last-minute edits so my first manuscript would read better and be more professional.

Special thanks to my family, who encourages me through the years to believe in my call and dream.

And most importantly, I want to thank my Lord and Savior Jesus Christ, who, when things seemed darkest, found amazing ways to renew my hope, increase my faith, and give me the physical, mental, and emotional strength to continue moving forward.

INTRODUCTION

After Diagnosis or unexpected news of:

A life-threatening or life-altering illness
A death
Financial reversal
Marital crisis
Some other life altering situation

Yes. There is life!

Yes, after the shock, there is *life*. And the life you discover may be the best you have ever known.

The journey, which caused me to write this book and develop The Life Givers Network®, began many years ago, but reached critical mass when my wife Paula received her breast cancer diagnosis. This book is not only for cancer patients. It's *not* merely for patients of any kind. It's for people fighting to live who confront various crises in life that stop us from living the life God has intended and planned for us. It's also for those who give an endless amount of love and caring, watching those they love struggle to hang on to life, and in the process often surrender the life they always hoped to live.

My most profound learning experiences come from dealing with many family and friends who had cancer and others confronting significant illnesses such as heart, ALS, MS, and Parkinson's. Nevertheless, the principles in this book help people deal with these issues. In one case, they helped someone who suffered the murder of a family member.

What you read is not rocket science. Instead, there is enough information and practical instruction to lead you from the point of devastation to extraordinary living. You can and will move toward an extraordinary life as soon as you implement the information contained in this book.

This material sets forth simple strategies and principles. These are the first steps my wife and I took to begin a new life in the face of impending mortality. Because of the success of these steps in my wife's life and the lives of many others, I developed The Life Givers Network®.

This information can radically transform your life and the lives of those around you. This program promotes a life filled with meaning and purpose, no matter how bad things seem. You may be thinking what lies ahead is a battle with illness when, in fact, if you allow yourself to find it, you discover a path to some of the best days you have ever lived.

While researching to help my wife, I read a line in one of my mentor's books about "singing the song you were created to sing," and it forever changed my life. It set me on the course to develop this program and seek ways to share this information with people in every community in America who want to live and experience God's help to live an extraordinary, not mediocre, life.

Out of what could have been the greatest tragedy in my life came a vision to bring hope and life to millions of people who face the greatest struggles of their lives. It's a vision that brings potential hope and radical life transformation to individuals, families, churches, businesses, and communities all over America. This vision offers a fresh perspective on why the people in our country need God.

Take your time. Move carefully through the material. Finish one chapter, then answer the questions at the end before you go on to the next. Expect to receive life-changing information before you get to the end. Dr. LeShan's book, *Cancer As A Turning Point*, surprised and blessed me. Reading this book may surprise you, but God will give you something for your situation that can radically change it. I believe that for you.

Let's start. Take a 3x5 card and write the words "Abundant Life" and "John 10:10" on one side. Put that card where you see it every morning and night. Meditate on what those words could mean for you. If you do that consistently for 30 days, your life will never be the same.

Start thinking and believing in *life*. No matter how bad your situation is, God wants to bless your life with a new *life* filled with meaning and purpose. He wants you to have an extraordinary experience. I can't wait to hear about your life changes.

How To Proceed

If you believe in God, understand God sets before you a choice—life or death, blessing or cursing—based on His word in Deuteronomy 30:19. God says, "Choose life." Whatever your situation looks like, choose to pursue life.

Ask God right now to show you that He is real.

In early 1972, I wasn't sure if there was a God and felt conflicted when confronted by a friend's dying child without answers for that family. If you're in a similar place, ask God to show you He is real.

In either case, do the following:

- Get a writing pad or spiral notebook with a pen or pencil.
- Read slowly and thoughtfully.
- Expect to think of new ways to live daily.
- Think about *life*.
- Believe in *life*.
- Take notes.
- Read one chapter at a time.
- Answer the questions at the end of each chapter.
- Don't move on until you've grasped the main points.

Now, take time to write at least one page, longhand, about what is happening in your heart and mind as you complete each chapter. If you feel led to write more than one page, do so while the ideas are fresh.

If you have questions, write me at life@tlgn.org.

This Is My Prayer For You:

Father God, I thank You that You made provision for the person holding this book to understand that You want to bring them abundant life according to John 10:10. Lord, whatever they believe right now, I pray You show them new and wonderful things every day for the next 30 days. You are the giver of life, the original "Life Giver." Lead each reader to the abundant life You want them to have. Amen.

CHAPTER ONE
BEGINNING

Where Should You Begin?

You or someone you care about received a life-threatening diagnosis, a life-altering illness, or some other crisis. As many have said, "Life will never, ever be the same." How right they are!

Speaking face-to-face, I'd say: "Let's cut to the chase and get to the hard points." A person with normal emotions, you would ask the same questions I asked when my wife, Paula, learned of her aggressive breast cancer: How bad is this going to be? How long will she live?

These and many other questions go through your heart and mind. But, please, let me grab your attention and say this: The battle beginning within

The battle beginning within you is primarily one issue, and it is not the illness. It is *Life* or death!

you is primarily one issue, and it is not the illness. It is *Life* or death!

Strangely, what happens when we hear such a diagnosis causes the focus to shift from the real question to another focal point—the struggle to conquer the disease.

God gives us a clear word to guide us. In Deuteronomy 30:19, He says, "I set before you this day, life or death, blessing or cursing. Choose *life* [emphasis mine]."

No matter how bad things may seem, no matter how bad the doctor's report, know this beyond any doubt: This is not the beginning of the end, but a *new beginning* if you allow it!

You may wonder, "How can you say that?"

First, my personal experience with my wife and fifteen other people in our family diagnosed with cancer made me believe in the possibilities. Secondly, thirty-eight years of ministry and counseling with some incredibly difficult situations taught me there is a new beginning no matter how bad it looks. At this point, you could not convince me otherwise.

For over two decades, since Paula's cancer diagnosis, I have been privileged to help people in seemingly impossible situations break barriers and live as never before. Many experiences contributed to shaping the Life Givers ministry. One of the most notable was my mentorship by Dr. Lawrence LeShan. Dr. LeShan is one of the foremost cancer researchers in the world. His insight about the countless patients he witnessed go into remission impacted every person in this work. His great faith that his patients would significantly improve their lives changed every person I meet.

Steven Covey, in his book *Seven Habits of Highly Effective People*, said all genuinely effective people begin with the end in mind. Sadly, most people start with the wrong end in mind. They focus on the experience of friends or family members who struggled and died or survived with a low quality of life. I did the same thing until my motivation changed to fight to help Paula. I believed everyone with cancer faced an early death.

Once I discovered someone could find a meaningful life in spite of a devastating diagnosis, my focus changed. This book is about what is possible and where to begin. In pursuing this, you learn there is more to *life* than the body!

This book is about what is possible and where to begin. In pursuing this, you learn there is more to *life* than the body!

You Are In The Right Place

In February 1991, a professor challenged me about taking healing to people intentionally. Like many in ministry, I waited for people to come to me. But what could be done about the "plague of cancer" around us? I felt powerless. Was I destined to watch people deal with cancer the same way and then die? The answer? NO!

God directed my steps to people who helped me see this differently. Reading the works of Dr. LeShan and meeting him personally, as well as studying the writings of men like Dr. Bernie Siegel, Norman Cousins, Dr. Carl Simonton, Dr. David Spiegel, and many others convinced me the impossible was possible.

I want you to discover that "the end" is not healing from some disease. Why? Because there will always be crises in your life. If not disease, it will be some other trouble. The *end* you look for and eagerly anticipate is the hope of *life*!

Few people attempt to accomplish their heart's desire. Many make their bucket list, but few plan and achieve what is on their list. Some people say they are afraid to make their list or are sure these things will never become a reality. Others look at me and say, "I can't go there."

While writing this, I spoke with a wonderful young woman who was in the hospital in Houston working on getting on the heart transplant list. A courageous single parent with a nine-year-old daughter, her pacemaker-defibrillator had to be replaced, as did her LVAD (left ventricular assist device). During our conversations, we spoke about what she would do if she had a new heart. Her list came quickly, including creative writing. When I asked if she had a pen, she called the nurse to bring her one. She grasped the importance of beginning her writing immediately and was she ever excited.

A few days after our conversation, a beautiful thing happened. A lady who had received a transplant visited the young single mom. The woman's new life, physically and otherwise, overflowed. This woman's eyes sparkled. Her excitement palpable in her voice. After her visitor left, my friend realized she had been lying around for five years, waiting to die. Her life difficult; she had little reason to expect things to change. But something did change that day. She wanted to be like the lady who visited her. Instead of a dread of dying, God gave her a new vision for life. He sent her a visual she understood.

After hearing her story, I told her how she encouraged me. Her doubt turned to the belief that life would be good. Awesome! She knew some things still must happen to get on the transplant list, but now she experienced a new life daily. Instead of hoping or wishing, she believed and received, which makes all the difference in the world. She saw "the end" change when her picture of death became her vision for life. Her darkness turned into light!

Although neither of us knows how or when this will happen, the story changes. As the prophet Hosea wrote, her valley of trouble transformed into a door of hope (Hosea 2:14,15). A remarkable thing took place in Houston!

> **Her valley of trouble transformed into a door of hope (Hosea 2:14,15).**

Do You See It?

Death turned into life. Hopelessness to hope. Darkness to light. John's Gospel says that darkness cannot overcome the light. Light always prevails. And so we have it. A young mother, lying in bed waiting to die, now lay in bed, experiencing a new sense of *life*.

This Can Happen To You

In the following pages, I share how you can see this same light come into your darkness, as it did in Houston, and begin your healing process. We base this on God's Word because what took place in these phone and hospital encounters cannot happen without supernatural intervention. The darkness in this world seeks to kill and destroy. The Light of the World brings hope and joy. As my friend got her life back, so can all who choose to put their trust in God.

In this book, I share with you six simple things my wife, Paula, and I did to fight off the darkness and get back into the light. Anyone can do these things. However, it's best not to do this alone. Find at least one person to walk with you, one with whom you can be honest and who won't tell you what to do.

These six things, explained in chapters two to seven, help you walk out the plan God has for your life:

- Responding to Diagnosis or Crisis
- Seeking God's help
- Evaluating your situation
- Making your plans
- Deciding on a course of action
- Beginning to ACT

Every step is simpler than you imagine. Don't make this complicated. Even your first step is simple and direct. If you understand what you've read, your task is clear: start thinking about how you want "your end" to look. And write down your thoughts.

About 97% of you believe you don't need to write things down. You think you'll remember them. This false belief is your first step toward failure.

FACT: only about 3% of healthy people do this.

The Bible says in Habakkuk 2:2, "Write the vision so you can run with it." God knows that when we pressed, we forget many things unless we wrote them down. But, when written, we are reminded often and able to run the race set before us (Hebrews 12:1).

Answer This Question

What is *life* to you? What do you want "the end" to look like? Here are some helpful questions:

- Is it a deeper, more intimate relationship with God?
- Is it fulfilling a call you've never acted on?
- Is it getting your family in order? Spending more

time with your spouse, children, and grandchildren?

- Is it healing some relationships?
- Is it being the best you can be in some field or endeavor?
- Is it writing a book? Painting a picture?

Life is more about quality than quantity. One young man who heard me speak recently told me he "got it" when I said, "Jesus lived 33 years." He prepared thirty years for His ministry of three. In those three years, he turned the world upside down.

After considering these questions, write your response in 20 words or less:

Life, for me, is _____.

Now, if you have not already done so, write the word *life* on a 3x5 card. Put it in a place where you can view it daily. You will make nine more of these cards, which will become your "lifeline" to the future. If you write, you moved into the top 2-3% of our society!

If you write, you moved into the top 2-3% of our society!

Tomorrow, when you wake with these thoughts on your mind, you wonder how you can go from where you are to where you want to be. Find at least one friend, possibly more, and tell them how you see what *life* can be. You don't need to know how you will get there. But, you need to know and believe it is no mistake you are reading this book, and things will be different.

In the past, when I heard about someone diagnosed with serious illness, I had certain images in my mind about what would happen next. After years of research and working with people one-on-one, I know the picture will be different. After getting information about individuals, I wonder what great things will happen in them, for them, and through them. This approach is radically different from what most people take.

I believe in a loving and merciful Creator who desires His creation to be all we were created to be. You may not agree with me for various reasons, but please, for your sake, keep an open mind.

In Chapter Two, I share how I began this process and how things changed. It took me years to learn this, which helps you move far ahead in your knowledge. You could do your research and spend years in the "school of hard knocks," or you can consider and embrace these eternal but straightforward truths that will forever change your life, and hopefully, other lives through you.

If you take what you've read up to this point, write it down, and run with it as I did in 1993, this is all you need. The rest of what you get here is like delicious icing on your cake.

The ball is in your court. If you feel new inner motivation, it is the Spirit of God encouraging you to move forward. Focus on what you read. Don't forget to write and daily review your writing. Carry your 3x5 cards. Be amazed at the thoughts that come to you, and how you are being led in ways you never imagined possible.

Your situation or physical condition may not change immediately, but you find your mind, heart, and attitude making major shifts. The Bible puts it this way:

Are you ready for the best days of your life? If not, get ready. The adventures begins.

"*Be transformed by the renewing of your mind . . . .*
(*Romans 12:1*)"

Become Aware

Have you written what the word *Life* means to you? If you didn't do it earlier, write your response now.

Life, for me, is: _____.

What keeps you from hoping you can experience this life?

If the disease or other crisis facing you were gone tomorrow, how would you live your life? What would you do first? What would be next? What keeps you from doing these things tomorrow?

Make Your Second 3x5 Card

Write on one side, "I'm in the top 3%."

Now, take the time to write at least one page, longhand, about your thoughts and feelings after reading this chapter. If you feel led to write more than one page, do so while the ideas are fresh in your mind.

It's time to move to Chapter Two.

CHAPTER TWO
RESPONSE OR REACTION

Stop Asking "Why?" Start Asking "What?"

These thoughts are from Psalm 112 (NKJV), which says: "Light arises in darkness for the upright . . . he will never be shaken . . . he will not fear evil tidings . . . his heart is established . . . he will not be afraid."

In the Introduction, I described what to do after being diagnosed with a life-threatening or life-altering illness or other crisis. You must *pursue life* with all your strength as your highest priority. Discovering this truth liberated Paula and me.

Once we identified our reasons for being, which took place during the darkest days we'd ever encountered, light arose. We knew we could grow and develop our lives in spite of evil trying to destroy all we knew. This clear awareness empowered us to live in the face of impending threats brought on by this illness. This short book communicates what has helped me, my family, and countless others find new life after receiving bad news.

In the years since 1992, I've learned how to get started as soon as possible. It's unnecessary to spend many weeks learning what to do. If you understand and apply some simple principles, you focus on the essentials and avoid the pitfalls. Learning from our experience should expedite your pursuit of *life* and significantly shorten your learning curve.

> This short book communicates what has helped me, my family, and countless others find new life after receiving bad news.

So, let's begin. In sharing my experience, I will be open and honest so you understand what happened in my life and what is possible in yours.

Every Person Has A Story

What does that have to do with anything? Well, it has everything to do with whether we are reactive or proactive, and how we do what we do.

For most, diagnosis is a complete shock, followed by the rapid and profound realization that life will never be the same. This shock paralyzes. Some people believe it was just a matter of time. Therefore, the diagnosis is inevitable. Then some know that life won't be the same, but are ready for the challenge. We were in this group.

Two years before her cancer diagnosis, Paula learned she needed gall bladder surgery. Her great pain and x-rays revealed a gall bladder loaded with stones. The surgeon advised quick action and scheduled surgery.

The results were amazing! When the surgery was over, the surgeon and our attending family physician came to me. They looked at each other and then looked at me. They were speechless. I asked what was wrong, but they remained silent. Finally, they said: "We don't understand. We couldn't find any stones. We know they were on the x-rays, and we double checked after beginning surgery, but they were not there."

I knew they were afraid of a lawsuit for unnecessary surgery. However, my only concern was that Paula was okay. This experience laid the groundwork for what we were to face two years later.

When we received the evil tidings of Paula's cancer, we had already experienced 17 years of great blessings from our faithful God. Since we knew He took the stones away (He is good at rolling stones away), we believed He would also remove the tumor. Though this did not happen, He showed us many new things, which built our confidence that, no matter what, He would care for us.

Our years of ministry taught us "the valley of trouble could become the doorway of hope" (Hosea 2:14-15). What a crazy thought, but God's ways are not ours. In our experience, trouble is not the end with God. Instead, problems often open a new door to fruitfulness and what the Bible refers to as "our vineyard." It was time to look for that fruitfulness, and what transpired surprised us.

> Our years of ministry taught us the "the valley of trouble could become the doorway of hope." (Hosea 2:14-15)

The Biopsy

One day Paula felt a lump in her breast. She informed me, and we looked for a doctor. Directed to one of the best breast specialists in our area, she made the appointment. We prayed, wholeheartedly believing God would either cause the lump to be benign or disappear.

When biopsy day came, we felt confident. Paula went to the operating room for the procedure while I waited. After she came out, we waited in the recovery area to speak with our doctor.

Watching him approach, the look on his face told us he had bad news: a malignant growth. We needed to make an appointment to discuss further steps.

Stunned and disappointed by this news, I embraced her then went to get the car, while the nurse brought Paula to the curb. As Paula entered the car, we looked at each other and remained silent all the way home. I used to think, and you might agree, that our silence was not a good thing. But now I see that it was very good. The Bible says in Psalm 46:10, "Be still and know that I am God . . .."

A million thoughts raced through our minds, some good, and some not so good. It was best our negative thoughts remained unspoken. What happened next would forever change how we faced every major crisis.

When we arrived home, we remained quiet for a while. Then I spoke, "I'll call our pastor and ask him and his wife to visit us." Having been set on a course we would not choose, we needed to share our experience and pray together. At that moment, we were perplexed and angry, with no idea what the outcome would be.

Speaking to our pastor, I briefly told him what happened, "We need you to come right away." He said they could not do that, and I said, "You don't understand. We need you to come now." They changed their plans and in a short while arrived at our house. For more than 90 minutes, we poured out our hearts. We expressed our anger, concerns about the future, and thoughts about our children. We understood cancer's previous impact on our family. Could we cope with this dreaded disease better than others? How would we do that? After listening patiently, our pastor and his wife moved the conversation to think about God and His faithfulness.

This challenged us. Since 1972 when I committed to serve God, we walked through many difficulties, but nothing like this. In every one, He had shown Himself faithful, so we had no reason to doubt Him now. What transpired in these moments was life-changing, which is why I love the testimony in 2 Chronicles 20:12, "For we have no power against this great multitude that is coming against us; nor do we know what to do, but our eyes are on You." God had to be our focus.

Our open and honest conversation changed our hearts. Although the passage referenced above was not yet part of my experience, God spoke to us that afternoon. We openly faced the serious nature of Paula's diagnosis. We discussed our thoughts and fears, what we felt about the future, and how powerless we were to do anything. In this situation, we were like Jehoshaphat. However, he did two more things. He declared aloud God's faithfulness to His people and then said, "We feel powerless against this enemy and don't know what to do, but our eyes are on you!" (2 Chronicles 20:12)

We poured out our hearts to one another, declaring the goodness and greatness of God in all situations. Though we had no idea what would come, we prayed and gave the whole thing to God. Then we experienced the most wonderful thing, which I regularly share with countless people since that biopsy in 1989.

Our pastor said, "Let's go eat a great meal and celebrate." That's what we did—went to a beautiful restaurant for a phenomenal meal. We celebrated life!

What a wonderful response to a horrible morning. Rather than having a pity party, we chose to celebrate.

Since 1972 I've watched people respond (or react) to bad news. Instinctively, people put their gifts to work, looking for a solution to their problems. With illness, they pull out all the stops and make phone calls because they don't know to turn, which is a very human reaction. They may do this with an air of confidence, but I know from talking with so many, fear of the future rules their thoughts. Many hesitate to share their real feelings with friends. They want to appear strong and self-controlled. God forbid we should lose control!

For many years I have said that to be forearmed is the best defense against formidable enemies. But are we ready for the things that come our way in life? Probably not. But what we did that day is the best preparation for any challenge. Let's be open and honest that we feel powerless and unsure about what to do. Then we can declare our assurance in the next step to fix our eyes on God.

You might wonder, "Is Jim suggesting I not to seek medical help?" On the contrary. Pursue the best medical help you can find. However, run to God first for help, asking His guidance and direction based on Matthew 6:33, which says, "Seek first the Kingdom of God and His righteousness and all these things shall be added unto you." God is interested in every detail in your life. He can show you the right doctor, treatment facility, protocol, or person to help in a crisis if you let Him. Why not try looking at things from God's perspective and see how different everything might be?

Run to God first for help.

Perfect Peace

In the full-length video, "The Life Giver Story," found on our website at www.tlgn.org, I noted that God gave us some outrageous promises. One of these is Isaiah 26.3: *"God will keep in perfect peace* the *one who is stayed (focused) on Him."* How outrageous is that? Our job is to stay focused; God's is to bless us with *perfect peace*. This peace is something most people cannot comprehend. They may observe it in those who know it, but as they watch us function at a high level, it is still a surprise.

This peace is one of the great benefits for those who turn to God first. Yes, in an emergency, we seek medical help at once. But even then, we look to God as we are on the way. We'll talk more about this later. What it means is we can have perfect peace in the storm as displayed by Jesus in Mark 4:35-39. This allows us to listen, think, and make better judgments about the next steps. If we are fearful, it's hard to make wise decisions. But if perfect peace is available, why would we refuse that gift?

Direction

One of the hardest things about dealing with a serious illness or other crisis is finding your way through the wilderness. As often as we hear the word cancer, each diagnosis begins a new story. How it will impact us and those near us remains to be seen. How we will respond to treatment, how our bodies will support our recovery, how our spirits will sustain us—these are all variables. We don't know until we *walk it out.*

Another thing that happens in our crisis is how many people want to tell us just what to do. Everyone seems to have advice. Some try listening to everyone or may listen to no one. Scripture says *there is wisdom in the multitude of counsel.* But who should we listen to? Our best answer is in God's Word. Proverbs 3:9 says, *"A man's mind plans his way, but the Lord directs his steps and makes his way sure."* No one else can make this promise. Why would we not want to look to God and let Him direct our way on a sure path?

Be Led To Life

God does help us *find life.* So often people are consumed with the physical process, missing *the things of life.* They become so obsessed with the body, the disease, the treatment, and other physical stuff they miss what is happening around them. They major in the *urgent* and miss the *most important things in life,* like relationships.

Life Givers has a Biblical base, a faith base that points people to God as the ultimate source of help and hope. Jesus says He came *so that we could have life, and have it in abundance* (John 10:10.) It is His greatest desire that we experience that life.

What Many People Do

If these simple things are true, why do so many try God only when they are in trouble? And I do mean *try.* When I meet people in crisis, I hear, "I think I'll try God." Whether you have a good relationship with God or little or none, the best response in a crisis is to turn to God first.

Several years ago, I helped a lady face a difficult diagnosis. Raised in the church, a Sunday School teacher for many years, she found herself in a unique place after her diagnosis. During her devotional times, she heard God say, "It's time to get serious with Me." What a shock that was. She was such a fervent Christian, but she said, "It's time."

Is it time for you to get serious with God, to let Him talk to you about your life? Do you need to tackle things from your past to which you responded, "Later, this isn't a convenient time"?

Do you remember my words: *the valley of trouble becomes the doorway to hope?* This hope can be for you if you put God first!

What is Your Response?

Are you ready to put God first, or will you say, "I have no time right now"? I hear those words often to which I respond, "You can't afford the luxury of not doing so." God wants to show you the way if you ask Him.

If not, He lets you work things out alone. If you want the One who can make your path sure, take time to write how you're going to respond to Him.

Become Aware

- What is God saying to me right now?

- What is going on in my life right now that is troubling?

- Am I angry? About what?

- Am I afraid? What is making me fearful? Be honest. Don't try to be spiritual.

- Do I feel overwhelmed and confused?

- Is God punishing you for something?

- Do I believe God wants me to have an abundant life?

Write your response to these questions and other things that come to mind.

Make card #3

Write, "I choose to celebrate 'what' is happening in my life."

Now, take the time to write at least one page, longhand, about your thoughts and feelings after reading this chapter. If you feel led to write more than one page, do so while the ideas are fresh in your mind.

CHAPTER THREE
SEEKING GOD FIRST

What Happens When I Seek God First

I didn't grow up in the Church. I didn't make a commitment to God until I was 27, married, had one child, and served overseas in the U.S. Army.

Why tell you this? I'm a deeply committed Christian, but was not indoctrinated by any particular denomination or sect. After almost 48 years of trouble, blessing, and seeking to know God through the Bible, I know that I know. God is real, and the only One we can count on. This foundation allows me to believe with all my heart that seeking God is the first thing to do when learning of a life-threatening or life-altering illness or some major crisis.

"Every Need" Addressed

In the summer of 1972, I followed Jesus. My commitment was to read the Bible, God's Word, and to understand what it meant to love God because He first loved me. This understanding sets forth Biblical faith in contrast to all religions. Then I learned that God tells me to seek Him first, and He'll provide my needs (Matthew 6.33). Another of the Bible's "outrageous promises." That summer, as I met with folks in our church for mid-week studies, my Biblical understanding increased. When I was asked to share my testimony about changing from being unchurched to being fervent in my faith, this was the verse I chose.

That evening in the fall of 1972 is still vivid in my memory. With no training in the Bible, having never attended Bible classes, and only a new church-goer, here I was talking with mature followers about a promise from God's Word. What a guarantee! If I sought God, He would supply all my needs. What an "outrageous" offer! As a new believer, with little Bible knowledge, nothing could have been more exciting. Who in this world could say, "Seek me, and I'll care for all your needs?" *No one but God.* Little did I know this would be one of the most important promises in my life.

Stop and think about this. My one aim was to seek God, not for anything special but solely for who He is. Then when I face some crisis, He promises to guide me on the right path. God does this because He knows me best. Think about it. Because He knows me best, He knows who to send me to, when and where to send me, and what to look for. He is my perfect guide. Knowing

> My one aim was to seek God, not for anything special but solely for who He is.

the beginning from the end, He would not experiment, but identifies my best course and provides for every need.

Let me illustrate. In 1994, just before our eldest daughter's wedding, Paula developed a wound under her arm. This was a result of her breast cancer. After diligent research, she found a breast specialist in a prestigious hospital in New York City. She made an appointment and went with a friend, hoping this doctor could help her, even if it required radical treatment.

After hours of examination, the doctor said, "I'm so sorry, but I can't help you." That news was bad enough, but she didn't stop there. As Paula rose from her chair to walk out, the doctor said, "There's one more thing. If I were you, I would go home and get my affairs in order, because I don't believe you will make it to the wedding." The wedding was only four weeks away! What a huge disappointment!

When Paula got back to New Jersey, she came directly to my office. She sat down on the sofa and began to cry. When I asked what was wrong, she responded, "The doctor can't help me." It seemed any earlier hope was gone, and she was devastated. What I didn't realize was how crushed Paula was by what the doctor said about not being able to make the wedding which she had not told me. We held each other for a few minutes, prayed, asking God what we should do. When we finished, I said, "We need to look for someone here (New Jersey.) She isn't the only doctor in the world." We did what I wrote about in the previous chapter. We asked God what was next. Paula went home to get the insurance information and begin another round of calls to find someone who might help.

Miraculously, Paula located a physician who was board-certified in four disciplines and had recently come to the hospital nearest us. She made an appointment and we went together. The cancer treatment center had newly opened, and this doctor was in charge of radiology. After examining Paula, he said, "Mrs. Henry, you have a challenging situation. I cannot make any promises, but I have been well trained and will use every bit of my expertise to help you. I know I'm limited in what I can do, but we'll do our best and trust God to do the rest."

Paula emerged from the examining room with a smile on her face. When I asked why, she said, "Let's go." In the car, she related what the doctor said about helping, his training and expertise, his limitations, and his desire to trust God for the results. "That was all I needed to hear," she said.

We had a doctor who knew he was an instrument through whom God could work. With his humility, we believed he would be a source of great help. Paula did make the wedding and lived on for two more years!

Personal Worth Is Validated

So many times in the past 20 years I've heard the words, "I don't want to be a burden to my family." While this sounds noble, upon further inquiry, it's easy to see their real thought is, "My life is not worth fighting for." How sad!

People like me, who found the truth later in life, were raised on false religion or no religion, are unable comprehend what God has done for us. We attempt to deny God sent His only Son to give His life for us. We find it too hard to explore the depth of that truth, because few would give their life for another. But that is exactly what God did for us.

News reports relate stories of people watching when someone is in trouble but doing nothing. This past year, a person lay dying on a New York City street, and no one bothered even to check on him. By the time someone stopped to help, it was too late. In another case, a lady sat in an emergency room waiting for help, but by the time they got to her, it was too late. So what do we do with the idea that someone gave His life for us?

God's action goes far beyond someone with humanitarian concerns for my health. The truth remains. God intends us to "have life and have it more abundantly." This is why Jesus gave His life for us. We are unique individuals who have a special place in God's creation. No other person out of the billions living on the earth has the same fingerprints or DNA. Why would this be so unless He wants us to know we are exceptional with a unique role in this world? If we fail to fulfill His purpose, our assignment will not get done.

Do we have value? Yes, beyond our comprehension. God's Word says we were created for good works before the foundation of the world (Ephesians 2:10). We need to discover what they are and walk in His Way. It further says we are fearfully and wonderfully made (Psalm 130). We're not accidents waiting to happen! Let me illustrate from the life of one who has been an integral part of Life Givers.

In 2004, God brought a wonderful lady named Diane into my life. A mutual friend told her I might be able to help with a personal family issue. One day I asked her, "What would you like to do with your life?" She had come to solve a problem, not discover God's plan for her life.

But, that day, she spoke about helping women in hard places. It was that simple. Not long after, Diane lost her job, which she didn't really like, and had difficulty finding another. I shared what was happening in our office and how our goal was to help people struggling with life-threatening illnesses. Little did Diane know how this would change her life. She put her skills to work on writing and editing our first publications: the Seeds of Life videos, workbook, and facilitators. She began using these skills to help her church, and soon after was hired as the Pastor's assistant. Diane helps countless numbers of people.

God's plan for Diane began with a single step of obedience and courage. Diane's willingness to accept my challenge to work with persons who had life-threatening illnesses became her door of opportunity. Had she not said yes, she would not have blessed so many. More importantly, her family members have been touched and ministered to because of her willingness to step out and take some chances by following God's leading.

Peace — Digging Deeper

Peace is one of the essential needs of everyone facing life-threatening or life-altering situations. In such a diagnosis, the words themselves send shock waves through the individual and family, unless people are in total denial. When people say, "Everything is fine," I know we have a problem. Everything is *not fine*. Life just got turned upside down and will never, ever be the same.

Now don't get me wrong. This crisis doesn't mean your life can't become better than you have ever known, but if you think you're going back to business as usual, you are in for a shock. Even though your diagnosis may be severe, within a brief time, you experience one of the most outrageous promises found in God's Word.

> Isaiah 26.3 says "You will keep him in perfect peace whose mind is stayed *on you.*"

Let these words sink in deeply. Isaiah 26:3 says, "You will keep him in perfect peace whose mind is stayed *on you*." You, the patient, have one job: to keep your focus on God. His responsibility is to keep you *in perfect peace*. Is this possible? Absolutely!

Why do you need peace? Your body needs peace so it can use its energy caring for its physical needs. When you are anxious and depressed, so is your immune system. Your body is weighed down with care, so it cannot respond to the crisis at hand. Frequently depressed persons experience sickness more often and have low levels of productivity. In contrast, when people have something to live for, their immune system is boosted and tends to heal more quickly.

You also need peace to be able to make wise decisions.

You also need peace to make wise decisions. When you are in turmoil, it is hard to concentrate, listen, think through options, and make choices. You become paralyzed, which is not good.

Peace is vital to have healthy relations with those around you. When you focus on treatments, pain, finances, and the like, connections with even those who are close become strained. Tensions rise, fear, bitterness, anger, and resentment begin to surface, and those involved are unable to talk about the essential things. Precious moments pass by, which cannot be recaptured.

There Is A Better Way

Let me share an example of how God gives us perfect peace amid a horrible situation. Around Valentine's Day 1996, Paula knew her treatments were doing no good. One Sunday, she asked me to call the oncologist the next day to set up a consultation. I complied, and we left for the appointment with great peace.

When we met with the doctor, not the one we had seen before, he asked rather smugly what we wanted. "You made this appointment. What do you want?" Paula replied, "My treatments are not working, and I want to stop. Just give me something to keep me stable or comfortable, whatever the case may be."

Puzzled by her remarks, he asked, "How do you know this?" She replied, "I know, because I know my body, and this stuff is not working." He then said she was right since the bloodwork came back and showed her cancer was going wild. From this moment forward, we experienced peace we had never known. Within weeks, I closed my office so we could be together for whatever time we had. God wonderfully provided some gifts, so we didn't need to worry about finances. And friends had given us the use of a Florida apartment so we could take one last vacation together.

We retraced the steps of our 25th-anniversary vacation, stopped at some East Coast spots we wanted to see, and then settled into our quiet spot on a small lake in St. Petersburg, Florida. We treasured those days filled with precious moments and sharing some of the best conversations ever. But as good as these days were, they were nothing compared to what our last few weeks were.

After two trips to the Emergency Room about six weeks before her passing, we knew the end was near. Either we would have a miracle, or Paula's "homegoing" would be soon. Yet, we had peace that surpassed all understanding. People who visited us commented that unless you knew someone in the house was dying, you would never know.

The dining room table always had goodies. Friends brought so much food I had to purchase a small refrigerator for the garage. Music and laughter filled the house with people sitting around the table, sharing, and encouraging one another and us. Unless you were there, it is hard to describe.

Even in Paula's last hours, incredible peace filled the house. At about 5:00 PM, when she looked at me, she struggled for breath. With her eyes fixed on mine, she said "I love you" one more time and slipped into a coma.

Our son Matt entered the room and wondered what to do. He was to graduate from college that weekend, and this night was his baccalaureate service. We looked at each other, and with peace and great calm, I heard the words, "You need to go. It's what your mom would want." He left, and about an hour later, his mom slipped into eternity.

Those last few months of our 34 years of marriage were some of the best, mostly because of our faith and trust in God. We received His perfect peace each day. While we sat quietly on a park bench in St. Petersburg, Florida, Paula made one remark, which became one of the most important things she ever said to me. We had visited a small local bookstore. While rummaging through the shelves, I discovered a book entitled, *The Artists Way* by Julia Cameron. My brief foray into the book before our time on the park bench stimulated a conversation about creativity. My wife taught our children music and crafts. I felt challenged in those areas. For that reason, I commented that I was not a creative person.

At that very moment, Paula had a surge of energy. She told me to look her directly in the eyes and said, "Listen to me, and don't ever forget this." Stunned, she spoke to me about my creativity and skill in helping people uncover their gifts and the reason for which they had been created. Paula's words that day became one of the key foundation pieces for The Life Givers Network®.

I believe this amazing Word was God's Word to me through my wife. It would not have occurred if we had not been living and walking in peace during the most painful days of our lives. You can experience this kind of peace by turning to God right now. Cry out to Him for help. He will answer and come to you. His Word says He is close to those who are brokenhearted. If you've not experienced His peace, invite Him to come into your life right now. Ask Him to forgive you for trying to do it all on your own (the Bible calls this sin, which is *thinking we know more than God*), and seek His help in what is likely the worst time of your life.

Become Aware

- Why should you seek God first?

- Do you know your true worth, which is your reason to live?

- Are you anxious, depressed, or suffering in private pain—in need of peace?

- Do you need to understand how God wants to help you?

- What needs would you like to see God address in your life?

We invite you to contact us. We want to help you find the way. Hopefully, answering these questions encourages you to make the first step.

Make card #4

Write, "I will seek to understand both what God wants and what He can do for me."

Now, take the time to write at least one page, longhand, about your thoughts and feelings after reading this chapter. If you feel led to write more than one page, do so while the ideas are fresh in your mind.

CHAPTER FOUR
WHAT'S REALLY IMPORTANT?

What Represents Life?

After reading the first three chapters of this short book, I hope you are on your way to a transformed journey and life. Armed with a new outlook, be encouraged that God wants to meet your every need. And you should be more confident because of the peace He offers you, and the value your life has to Him.

Now it's time to face the hardest part of this process: *being real and honest*. Unless you are real and honest, the whole exercise fails. When what you say and what you believe differs, this inner conflict produces stress, which diminishes the effectiveness of your immune system.

You know that even when you are healthy, believing one thing and saying another affects mental, emotional, and physical energy. You need all the strength you can muster to battle for your health. What's vital to your well-being is the priority. All other concerns come later. Your spouse, family, and friends will likely sacrifice to care for you in the days ahead.

Let me illustrate. When Paula and I did research about how to approach treatment, she also wrestled with the course our lives now took. We served God and His Church for 17 difficult years. Don't get me wrong. We had incredible times, but the practicalities of life were hard—minimal pay, modest housing and clothing, limited nights out. But our Disney trip, tied to a ministry trip, was an absolute miracle.

> **What's vital to your well-being is the priority.**

In the summer of 1990, after 18 years of serving and sacrifice, I was laid off from a staff position and had no idea where to turn. We had four children—a daughter in her senior year of college, a son entering grade 12, a son with learning disabilities, and my youngest starting high school. My wife faced her first cancer surgery. The layoff overwhelmed Paula, the straw that broke her patience and longsuffering.

One night she blurted out, "I can't do this anymore!" When I asked why, she responded, "I can't live in a fishbowl any longer." Things changed quickly that night. Paula referred to life as a pastor's wife, for which I spent the previous 18 years preparing. What to do? I was shocked. When I asked, "How long have you felt this way?" her reply shocked me even more. "From the beginning," she responded. From the day we left for seminary, she had serious concerns about our calling, but never voiced them.

Again, what to do? Reviewing my training and experience over these years, I wondered what we might do. Reflecting on our experience for the previous two years about how people could have the best chance of fighting their illness and living a meaningful life, I knew the answer. No matter how much time and energy it took, I had to lay aside my dreams and focus on helping Paula identify and fulfill hers. Strangely, being a pastor's wife was her only identity, and she had just lost this. We were starting from scratch—both of us!

Being Real—Don't Wait

Don't wait until you face your mortality to express your honest opinions. To us, the explanation was clear and straightforward: Paula honestly believed that to be a good pastor's wife, she should follow my calling. Because she now spoke frankly, we could find where we belonged, which was good and necessary for the battle ahead.

The next six months were tough, but I used my teaching and speaking skills to provide some income while we sought God's next assignment. In the spring of 1991, God's call came "to do something about this cancer thing" while I was completing a graduate-level course work. Although unsure of what this meant, the call was clear. I knew this was for me, not both of us. On this, we agreed.

> Don't wait until you face your mortality to express your honest opinions.

It took ten months, but by the end of 1991, we had plans to open a center that would address the spiritual and emotional needs of cancer patients and their families. We began by working with churches with whom I had relationships. We would see how God would use my pastoral gifts and training in this challenging area of ministry.

Letting God Lead The Way

While we prayed for wisdom about how to fulfill this calling, we also sought something to bring purpose and excitement into Paula's life. Soon her call came. Suddenly and unexpectantly, a friend called one day. When Paula answered, the caller said, "I hear that you give piano lessons." Although she was not giving any and had no plans to do so, she responded with one word, "Really?" When asked if she would teach this friend's daughter, she said, "Yes," and launched her new career!

A few years before, just after I started seminary, Paula thought about enrolling in college. Asbury College was nearby, and with both of us in school, we had a high likelihood of financial aid. But she never liked high school, and her grades reflected this. Nevertheless, Asbury accepted her on probation, and her A's and B's were a blessing to us. Little did we know that God was preparing her for the best, most productive days of her life.

A few months later, that same friend called to say the music teacher at her daughter's school was going out on maternity leave. Paula's name was submitted as a candidate, which seemed impossible. She only finished a year and a half of college and had no certificate, but was an excellent teacher. As a Catholic School, they were not bound by the same laws. They interviewed five or six candidates, and Paula got the job! For the next three years, Paula taught music in four schools, to about1,200 students. She conducted numerous winter and spring concerts and taught 40 students in our home. When the senior principal learned we needed health coverage, she assigned Paula enough hours to qualify. This insurance paid all our medical bills, and covered her for disability when she had to stop teaching. These were truly miraculous days.

We both needed ways to bring new meaning and purpose to *our lives.*

What Did We Learn From This Experience?

Let me summarize:

- The patient had high priority.
- We had to agree. The Bible teaches that two cannot walk together unless they be agreed (Amos 3:3).
- We both needed ways to bring new meaning and purpose to our lives.
- To fight effectively, we needed to express what brought us joy and fulfillment.
- How we live from day to day is a true expression of why we are created and brings zest to our lives.

Our gifts were present, but lying dormant. They needed to be identified, stirred up, and put to use. When we engaged in doing things we enjoyed, life came back to our house in spite of the grave illness confronting us daily.

To move forward, we discovered issues to address about which we had not previously concerned us. Here are a few of them.

Toxic Influences

Before dealing with Paula's life-threatening illness, I did not see how many people in my life were actually "toxic." People who were such negative influences, draining our time, spiritual, mental, and emotional energy, leaving us exhausted at the end of visits. As we examined all areas of our lives, it became quite clear that if we were sincere, quite a few people, activities, and things in our lives were not good for us. But the most difficult word in the English language for the majority of us is "No."

The Bible teaches that "as we think, so are we" (Proverbs 23.7). The Book of Romans in the New Testament, verses 12:1,2 tells us to renew our minds, but few of us understand this. The mind is powerful, and this is important when fighting illness. This concept struck me when I read medical reports about testing by leading institutions and physicians.

One study by a prominent physician described patients who thought they were receiving a new drug to help prevent nausea during chemotherapy. The drug was given, the treatments administered, and not one of these people was nauseous. The medication b given was to induce vomiting. The suggestion by the leader of the study, that no one would be nauseous, caused their minds to override any other effect. The mind is incredibly powerful!

So, be on guard against the following:

- Toxic family members and friends
- TV shows
- Internet
- News programs
- Magazines
- Books
- Health care workers
- Church members

In a few words, someone can impart a thought that can take a person months, even years to recover from! Think about this contrast:

Doctor One says, "I'm sorry to tell you, it doesn't look good." He establishes a bad scenario, if not a death sentence.

Doctor Two says, "We've run the tests, and you *do have* _____, but we have several ways to approach this." The patient is ready, along with the doctor, to choose the right option and begin to fight.

Another area where you need to take a hard look is:

- Small Groups

  These might be church, hospital, or organization-based. While many small groups are beneficial, there are people in groups who say, "I went to that group depressed, and came out more depressed." Many stay away from groups because of negative people, negative conversations, people who are too happy, and being required to talk. These people want help with real emotional or spiritual issues that many groups usually will not touch. They fear to be with other sick people, especially those facing imminent death. I've known of grief groups that encourage more grieving than healing.

  This is critical to your well-being. Whether you are in a support group, Bible study, or something else, be careful to choose a group that focuses on life, growth, and positive attitudes. Avoid people who have a pity party or talk about things that depress and discourage.

Everyone needs a personal support group, but particularly those battling life-threatening illness.

- Personal Support Team

  Everyone needs a personal support group, but particularly those battling life-threatening illnesses. Most people do not have this kind of support. Women are more likely to be part of a group, but men are more reluctant and, in general, have few friends. When it comes to serious illness, many of us want to live in the land of denial. We say, "I'm fine" in public, but when confronted, we admit our fears. Why is this?

  It is mostly a matter of safety—the fear of being rejected. A healthy way to overcome fear is to voice that fear out loud. However, too often, when you do, you feel judged, inept, or have your feelings devalued or minimized. If so, you will zip your lip and hold on to negative feelings. These negative emotions become like cancer in your system, suppressing your immune system, and hindering your healing.

  Because of this, we need support teams who come around the patients to encourage them toward holistic healing. This support is not to adjust the patient as some see it, but to be present to encourage this person to make wise and healthy choices. And this support team needs to be helping the patient accomplish what is in their heart. They are not present to impose their own ideas which they think are best for the person.

- Worship

  A final but vital area to consider and evaluate is *where you worship*. In the video, you heard that the Bible declares God's Word to be ". . . *life to those who find them and health to all their flesh* (Proverbs 4.22)."

People talk of the place of worship as *a sanctuary*, and that's what it should be. A sanctuary is a place of peace and rest, where we hear about the greatness and goodness of God. In His presence, any problem becomes small. So, the sanctuary is the place to be refreshed and strengthened for the week ahead. It should be a place of joy, peace, and vision for life.

Sadly, this is not true in many American churches. Instead, people *fight* about trivial things. Often our churches are led by pastors who are discouraged and disheartened. With membership declining, **We should have peace and rest in His Presence.** finances are a struggle, and conversation often centers on *how to keep the doors open*. This struggle doesn't mention the battle between factions in the congregation, or between the pastor and the people. This is not God's intention for His church.

What God intends is this: In His Word we will find all we need. We should have peace and rest in His Presence. We should hear words that build our faith, and encourage, strengthen, and edify us. Our sanctuaries should be places where there is a river that never, ever runs dry. Since God is *"our refuge and strength, a very present help in trouble,"* (Psalm 46:1) we can call on Him in the day of trouble and find strength for today and tomorrow.

Therefore, we carefully evaluate if our place of worship is conducive to health *and healing* for life and godliness. Many of us choose a church based on family tradition, convenient location, the form of worship, denominational preference, and the like. The Bible says we join the Body where God wills. If your church does not present a Sovereign God, who is bigger than any problem, and cares for you in all things, you need to find another place of worship. An alternative is to seek, by God's grace and power, to bring renewal in your own church.

When we face serious crises, men or institutions will fail us. In those times, we need somewhere to turn for help. Hebrews 4:16 says to "...*come boldly to the throne of grace in time of need.*" You need to know how to find that place or seek help from others.

Now, take some time for the hard work. Write down the things that have come to your mind as you've been reading this chapter.

Become Aware In Light Of Material In This Chapter

- Do you love what you do on a daily basis?

- What would you do differently if you had only months to live?

- What relationships would you change?

- What groups would you leave? Try to join?

- If you started a group, what would it be like?

- How well does your church exalt God and strengthen you?

Record the facts. You get the idea. You're on the way.

Make card #5

Write, "I'm nurturing healthy things and removing toxic things from my life."

Now, take the time to write at least one page, long hand, about your thoughts and feelings after reading this chapter. If you feel led to write more than one page, do so while the ideas are fresh in your mind.

CHAPTER FIVE

PLANNING

What Is Most Important? What Do I Need To Begin?

If you've gotten this far, and have your thoughts, ideas, and answers to questions written down or in your computer, you are in the top 3% of people in America.

One research study said only 3% of all people write their vision, goals, and plans to achieve them.

One research study said only 3% of all people write their vision, goals, and plans to achieve them. But let's go back to the premise that we are going to commit our plans to God and ask Him to direct us. Listen to these words from Habakkuk 2:2:

> *Write the vision and make it plain on tablets, that he may run who reads it. For the vision is yet for an appointed time; but at the end it will speak, and*

*it will not lie. Though it tarries wait for it; because
it will surely come, it will not tarry.*

Whether you were diagnosed recently with an illness, or are in the thick of the battle, the principle applies. Stop, get some paper, and write. You might say, "I don't need to write. I'll keep it in my head."

Napoleon Hill, who studied the lives of the most successful men in the early 1900's, noted that those who write their plans are ten times more likely to accomplish their objectives. Therefore, why not write? If you don't:

- You soon forget ideas that come in a flash.
- You waste time trying to remember them.
- You allow unimportant things to consume your time.
- You won't follow God, who is trying to help you. He would not have told us to write things down unless He knew we needed to do so.

So where does one begin?

Begin By Making A List

Go back to your evaluation and make a list. You may have tried this before and found it to be complicated. But the process should be much easier this time because if you were honest during your evaluation, you discovered some things you used to think important are removed from your list. It's quite amazing.

When your life is threatened, essen-

> Napoleon Hill noted that those who write their plans are ten times more likely to accomplish their objectives.

tial things jump off the page. You can't wait for some

tomorrow, which may never arrive. It becomes simple, yet so profound. You feel compelled to take action.

Years ago, I discovered a little book entitled *The Tyranny of the Urgent* by Charles Hummel, published by InterVarsity Press. His main point is *every day of our lives we are pressed by "tyranny" that is caused by urgent things. So we often neglect the crucial things.* It's the main reason many of us fail to accomplish the things we want in life. We cater to the urgent and neglect the important.

> **According to Charles Hummel, every day of our lives we are pressed by "tyranny" that is caused by urgent things. So we often neglect the crucial things.**

Based on your work in Chapter Four, would you list ten or more things you want to do if you know your days on earth are short? You probably thought about these for years, but delayed them, thinking "I'll get to that one day." That day is here. It is now!

Write down the ten things you want to accomplish if you only had six months to live. Don't be surprised if your list grows beyond ten. That's okay. Identifying the things important to you is good.

Keep one thing in mind as you write: List the activities that make you fully alive. Remember the goal: moving toward a meaningful purpose-filled life.

Organize Your List

When you finish your list, review it, and identify the major categories (e.g., your spiritual life, family, work, and legacy). I suggest no more than seven categories. Now, look at your list and place each item into one of these categories.

At this point, stick with gathering facts. Don't ana-
lyze your data; just collect information. Let your list sit
for a day or two. As the days go by, you may want to add
or remove some items once you see how helpful this is.

Choose The Top Ten

It may take a week or more to create your list, but this
time is invaluable. When you have your list completed,
select your top ten. What gives you the most joy and
makes you feel the most alive?

It's Story Time

At this point, some of you think, "I can't do this right
now." You are busy and under stress. So, let me share
two stories.

Recently a business leader who attended one of our
planning sessions told me this incredible story. As a
board member for *Make a Wish Foundation*, as they
made dreams come true for children, they confronted
an unusual issue. Some of the children taking their trip
of a lifetime returned
home and got better.   **When people focus on *life***
Can you imagine?   **instead of illness, miracles happen**
    It proves what   **every day.**
Life Givers has been
talking about for years. When people focus on *life*
instead of illness, miracles happen every day. They are
a reality, not an illusion.

Here's a second story. I officiated Mike's wedding.
When his wife of only a few years died, deeply depressed,
Mike could hardly function.

One day while riding his bike, he was hit by a truck. In the next 18 months, Mike had seven or eight surgeries and constant therapy. When I talked with him about getting his life back together, he said he didn't have time. He was right. Mike had become what I call a "professional patient." Though this was the first time I used this term, I've used it many times since. Mike saw various doctors to plan the next surgery to heal his body.

Meanwhile, he was dying inside. Life had ceased. He was like a robot going from appointment to appointment.

One day I had had enough and said, "Mike, this has to stop. You've got to cut out one of your appointments, and if it has to be me, so be it. But you must do something to get your life back." The lights went on. Mike took one day a week for himself and reclaimed his life. So can anyone facing acute trauma and deep depression.

Back To The Top Ten

As you review your Top Ten list, separate your items into the *short-term* and *long-term*. Choose something you can start *now*. Put that on the top of your list. Then select items which you can begin in the next two to three weeks, the next two to three months, and finally within a year. Making this list energizes you. You experience what we talked about earlier from Habakkuk 2:2 ". . . write the vision so you can run with it."

When you do this, you see your energy level increase. There is nothing like *having something to live for* when you awaken in the morning, something bigger than you. You may have only minutes to follow your dreams, but those are minutes you long for. You won't know how good this is until you do it. Now ask yourself another question.

What Do I Need To Accomplish My Dreams?

As you review your ten items, assume money is no hindrance. List every resource you need to accomplish them. You may have everything you need already. Others may need human as well as other resources, including money. Write them down now. If you're stuck and can't write because you're thinking "Why bother, this won't happen," read this story:

I'd known Carol for years. But seven years before her 27-year battle with cancer ended, she called me and said, "it" was back and she felt she could no longer walk this alone. Would I walk this out with her? Soon after our conversations began, we centered on the things she wanted to do most. I suggested she make a list. Before we spoke again, her list was complete.

Very near the top of her list was her desire to see some inspiring places and take photos. Financially, this was impossible. However, before we met to discuss which item she wanted to work on, Carol received an amazing call. Her best friend and her husband talked. They offered to pay for Carol and her friend to go anywhere in the world. The two women made three choices. One place was on both lists. So they headed for the Pacific Northwest. She sent me a framed photo of the most beautiful scene from that trip.

God made her impossibility possible! And what joy and energy it produced. Not only did she see an awe-inspiring place, but she published a book with scriptures and her photos. I have a copy in my office.

Carol left her mark in the many lives she touched before her passing.

Don't limit God! *If you haven't made your list, do it now!*

When you have completed your list, take the time to write next to each item what you need to accomplish it. If, like Carol, it is a trip that inspires you, estimate everything required to make the trip happen.

If You Haven't Made Your List, Do It Now

Be specific. Know where you want to go, how long you want to stay, and what you want to see. Do you need a new camera to capture highlights? New luggage? Who will accompany you? When do you need to make reservations? Think about this. Then, write it down. See yourself there. Now, move on.

Consider each of your ten items. What do you need to make each happen? Remember, not everything you want is costly. Some won't cost you anything but time. Begin with these.

I love Goethe's quote, "Beginning has genius in it." Why? Because when you begin, your mind takes you to another level. Things you may have forgotten, or never thought of before, come to mind. You think creatively. Then you find God is creative and brings you what you don't expect, which blesses you beyond imagination.

Grow Your Team

Consider creating a safe, supportive team to walk with you through this experience. One reason for this is that your energy level may be low, and your thinking not as clear as usual. Don't be reluctant to ask for help. Don't let your pride get in the way and say, "It's okay. I can handle this myself." Don't waste precious time doing tasks others could help with. Focus on more important things. Don't let the urgent crowd out the important.

Give serious thought when choosing your team. You don't need people who tell you what to do. You need folks who help you accomplish your dreams and live. You need creative people who believe in miracles and think beyond your apparent limitations. Notice, I said, "apparent."

Don't be reluctant to ask for help. Don't let your pride get in the way. Don't waste precious time.

Who are these people? Your spouse, of course, who hopefully is your chief supporter. Choose friends who will wrestle through spiritual issues with you. You need people who know you and the Bible, understand your beliefs, and can help you grow positively without offending you. Think about someone to help you with nutrition, so your body will do what it was created to do. We cover this area more in recordings and on our website. And have on your team a *practical person* who can coordinate people to help with work, meals, things around the house, and whatever is needed.

Finally, make sure you have at least one "close, trusted friend." You need a friend in whom you can confide without judgment or criticism. This person is one you love and respect, who can hear anything from you without being shocked, and who is always available. Let me illustrate.

In the late 1980s, I met a man named Chris Larson. During our meeting, I noticed something very special about Chris. He was blind, but had more in*sight* than most people. Because of his sight-loss, his fine-tuned hearing and thinking allowed Chris to speak life-giving words. His approach was unique, and I wanted to know him.

In team building, look for seasoned people. What do I mean? When Chris and I met privately for the first time, he shared where he had been in life and how he came to this moment. He experienced enough trauma and tragedy to make anyone bitter and resentful. A drunk driver killed his daughter, he lost his eyesight, and his wife died in his arms. But Chris was one of the most gentle, giving, and forgiving spirits I ever met. For over 14 years, Chris and I spoke nearly every day. We gave each other no more than 10 minutes to have a pity party. Then we would say, "It's time to move on." This habit was so healing for both of us. Chris' picture hangs *on my office wall along with one of his favorite white walking canes, and a hat with a logo: Relax. God's in Charge.* Every day that picture reminds and challenges me about the meaning of real friendship.

In team building, look for seasoned people.

Then there is my wife's friend Linda. Special friends, we enjoyed many hours with Linda and Tony. In the days before Paula's death, Linda visited family in England. When Paula's passing seemed imminent, we tried to reach Linda. Learning she didn't have a flight until the weekend, we were concerned she would not get home to see Paula one last time.

Relax. God's in Charge.

Much to our surprise, Linda called her family, saying she changed her flight and was on the way. Coming directly from the airport, Paula was delighted to see her.

When Linda left, I asked, "What is so special about this relationship?" Paula's immediate reply was, "That's easy. She calls me every day and makes me laugh." Paula could have no better medicine, especially when the man-made medication was ineffective. These friendships get us through the most challenging times.

Before moving on to the next chapter, do the following work.

Become Aware

Reflect on these questions:

- Do you have a notebook to write your vision?

- What things are important as opposed to urgent?

- What are your major categories?

- What is your "top ten"?

- What is needed to do each item?

- What people do you want on your team?

Make card #6

Write: The major parts of my plan include (write steps here).

Now, take the time to write at least one page, longhand, about your thoughts and feelings after reading this chapter. If you feel led to write more than one page, do so while the ideas are fresh in your mind.

CHAPTER SIX
DECISION TIME

What Is Your Next Step? What Is The Most Important?

In Chapter 5, you worked on your plans. In the process, some things stood out more than others. Ask yourself: *If I could only do one of the ten things, what would it be?*

Think about both short and long-term effects. What brings you the most joy if you began today? What would have the most lasting impact on your life and in the lives of those closest to you?

Ask yourself: If I could only do one of the ten things, what would it be?

Put the matter of money aside for now. Thinking in terms of limitless resources will help you decide what is most important to accomplish.

When you have decided on what is your Number One, then apply the same process to determine your

Number Two. Repeat this until you have ranked all your goals from one to ten.

What Is Next?

We'll return to your list, but first, get out your planner. If you don't have one, get one. Or at least use a month-at-a-glance calendar. Mark the dates where you have commitments. Once again, we are talking about the *urgent* versus the *important*. The *urgent items loom large*, but are usually less significant in the long run compared with *the important ones.*

> The urgent items loom large, *but are usually far less significant in the long run compared with the important ones.*

Franklin Covey has excellent resources, including *What Matters Most* by Hiram Smith. Mr. Smith brilliantly illustrates how to put the most rocks into a jar. First, set in the larger ones. Then progressively add the smaller ones, and finally the sand fills all the space between the rocks. You handle life the same way. If you put the small stuff in first, you have no room for the large, more important items. Does this sound familiar? It's why we often get to the end of the week and say there weren't enough hours to get everything done.

Don't get discouraged if you don't seem to have enough time for what's essential. Just begin! Plan some time to work on *What Matters Most*, if it's only an hour a week. As you do, you get more excited about this and want to allocate more time to *the important*. It's amazing. You want to give more time to those things from which you draw strength and emotional energy. *This tactic does work.* You always return to the things you enjoy. Now you have permission to remove some urgent but less important things. You've just begun.

Now, Back To Your List

Look at your list again. Identify significant blocks of time for *important things.* Start small by finding free time slots and writing in something like *my time.* Remember, you need to work on this. Your schedule will be in a state of flux for some time.

When you find blocks of time, review your list. Now the process gets a little harder. So let me help make the decision process a bit easier. As you work on things that are *important,* you may hear "Are you sure you should be doing this now? Aren't you a bit selfish? Shouldn't you be doing something else first?" Let's set the record straight here. The Bible teaches: *Love the Lord your God with all your heart, with all your soul, with all your strength, and love your neighbor as you love yourself.* For me, the message in these words is love God first, then yourself, then others. This message differs a bit from what many say, but let me explain.

If you are not in love with who God made you, it is tough for you to love and appreciate others whom He has made. Often, we feel frustrated we can't do what others are doing, which skews our rela-

If you are not in love with who God made you to be, *it is very hard for you to genuinely love and appreciate others whom He has made.*

tionships. Some people say, "hurt people hurt people." So take God at His word. Your prime time should be His, through worship, Bible study, prayer, and fellowship with His people. Then you make time for yourself, with the focus on *important things.* Finally, serve your neighbor and others the Lord puts in your path. This focus takes most of your time. But don't be concerned. As you reorient your life, you will make continual adjustments and remove unimportant things from your life as you prioritize *important things.*

When you begin, people will question you. People you care for may want your attention, and won't understand why you spend so much time on yourself. When Paula and I reoriented our lives, people challenged us. But when they saw us enjoying life in a difficult situation, they were a bit jealous (in a good way) and wanted to know our secret. So, please God and listen to His voice, care for yourself and each other, then care for others as He directs and provides the time.

Give Yourself Permission—Huge!
Permission To Talk

You have permission to do things in life. When facing critical issues, it's funny what happens to our decision-making process. People become acutely aware of things in the category of what do I have to lose? Things we once feared, we fear no longer. If faced with a serious illness, it's amazing how most people relate, knowing how sick you are. I've watched people with terminal diagnoses develop great boldness long before they leave this earth.

They often joke about how hard it is to deny a dying person the right to speak. Talk about freedom of speech.

This doesn't mean you may be rude or disrespectful. It does mean you likely have more of a hearing than ever, so take advantage of it. However, don't be selfish. Trust God to lead you through these days, and take you places you may have never been before. Don't say, "I can't do this." So many people I've spoken to over the years have said that. This may be your time—time to dream, plan, and do what you thought impossible.

It's amazing what you begin to think, if you permit yourself.

You may accomplish more than you ever dreamed. And the very process of living your dreams may send your body the message, "I don't have time for this disease." Your body may begin doing what God created it to do—heal itself. My oldest son, also a cancer patient, said many times, "I don't have time for this. I'm too busy living."

> This may be your time—time to dream, plan, and do what you thought impossible.

Permission To Dream

What we do begins in the heart and mind, with a dream, resurrecting the hope of doing something we gave up long ago. God affirms in Psalm 27:13: "I would have fainted unless I believed to see the goodness of God in the land of the living." When I realize the God of the impossible is with me, and He wants me to see His goodness, my hope is restored.

No one can live without hope. The Bible says, "Hope deferred makes the heart sick, but a desire that is on the way is a tree of life." (Proverbs 13.12) We don't need to see the manifestation of the things we hope for, but to know it is on the way. This knowledge brings hope, which becomes "a tree of life." Its fruit is *life*, in

> The Bible says, "Hope deferred makes the heart sick, but a desire that is on the way is a tree of life." (Proverbs 13:12)

every sense—spiritual, mental, emotional, and physical. That is fantastic news!

How do I know this works? Soon after opening my office in 1992, I met a young man who recently learned he had only two months to live. On our second visit, he shared his hopes and dreams for his family, things he had not told anyone. These dreams unleashed creativity and a new fight in him.

Will you permit yourself *to dream?*

This young man explored new possibilities for treatment and everything else in his life. As a result he lived for about 18 months. He experienced amazing victories during that time. God did far beyond what he could ask or think.

Will you permit yourself to dream?

Permission Regarding Relationships

We all have difficulty with relationships. But we often fail to see the toxic ones until pressed for time. When confronted by our mortality, we realize certain people are a real drain. Now we recognize the hard work we must do. We must learn to say, "No." In those situations where we wanted to say no but never did, we must say, "I'm sorry, but I don't have time now." Learning this skill is so liberating we wonder why we waited so long.

On the positive side, we permit ourselves to spend more time with those we choose. What joy this brings— saying "yes" and saying "no"! It transforms our entire life.

Permission To Worship

Now I'm going to meddle. Since hearing God's voice is vital in this process, it is critical to remove all obstacles. What are the implications for this?

When you are fighting for your life, the last thing you need is to worship in a place where you leave more depressed than when you entered. How can this be? After 48 years of ministry, I know many churches where there are undertones of conflict when people gather. This conflict should not be, and it is certainly no place for a person who is in the middle of a battle for their life.

Your church should be a sanctuary. I alluded to this earlier in Chapter 4. When you are fighting for your life, think about what you get from your place of worship. You should hear about a God who is so much bigger than any issue in life. You should find peace, hope, encouragement, and genuine friends who are supportive, not patronizing. You need a pastor who cares for you, knows you, and understands what you are experiencing. You need a "house of prayer" where people faithfully pray and have answers to their prayers. And you must hear a message from God's Word that gives you direction and strength for what lies ahead. If these are not your experiences, why worship there?

> You should hear about a God who is so much bigger than any issue in life.

Many are in a church because it is their denomination, where their family has always attended, or is convenient. Many can't tell you what they believe or why. However, if you are in a battle for your life, you find a church that fully supports you. It is imperative to be in a fellowship that proclaims God's Truth in word and deed.

Permission To Believe

You must be sure of what you believe about yourself and your God. Long ago, I found a book by Paul Little entitled *Know What You Believe and Why*. This book title speaks volumes. When people are diagnosed with a life-threatening illness, some have one problem, others have two. Unbelievers have one issue, their illness. Believers usually have two—first, a problem with the disease and, secondly, a problem with God.

Christians want answers. They seek the best medical care, but also want answers to their spiritual questions created by the illness. Why, God, has this happened? What are you teaching me? Why don't you answer my prayers? Do you know this impacts me, my family, and my future? And the list goes on.

Turn to God's Word, the Bible. For some, it's a book with stories, some true, some fictional. Fewer carry their Bibles to church. Even fewer believe it's true. But you must seek a place where Scriptures are the source of *all* we need for life and Godliness.

When Paula began her battle with breast cancer, a lady named Dodie Osteen told the world how God miraculously healed her. Her husband John confessed it was Dodie's faith in God's Word that brought her through her battle with liver cancer.

As stated in Proverbs 4:22, the words of God are "life to those who find them and health to all flesh." Again, we encounter conflict. Many today say we can't know what God wants to do. But after nearly five decades in ministry, I've learned that when you love someone, you come boldly to God on his or her behalf.

> As stated in Proverbs 4:22, the very words of God are "life to those who find them and health to all flesh."

Many years ago, I heard about a lady diagnosed with terminal cancer. She asked her pastor if the elders would pray for her healing, as taught in James 5:16. Her pastor said he was sorry, but they didn't believe that part of the Word of God. She went to other church doors, seeking someone who did believe that verse. Finally, she found a pastor who said, "Yes." She made an appointment, the elders anointed her with oil, and she was healed. She wanted to obey God's Word.

Become Aware

As you think about the things you've just read, answer these questions:

- What do you need?

- Do you need affirmation?

- Do you need physical healing?

- Have you read or heard a promise from God you'd like to believe?

- Do you have at least one person who would believe with you?

The Book of Hebrews tells us that, "He who comes to God must believe that He is, and that He, God, is a rewarder of those who diligently seek Him (Hebrews 11:6)."

Why not believe God's Word and its outrageous promises?

Make card #7

Write, "I choose to believe I can accomplish my highest priority which is (write it here)."

Now, take the time to write at least one page, longhand, about your thoughts and feelings after reading this chapter. If you feel led to write more than one page, do so while the ideas are fresh in your mind.

CHAPTER SEVEN
ACT

Years ago, I read this quote from Johann Wolfgang von Goethe, world famous German writer, which is still relevant today:

> *The moment one definitely commits oneself, then Providence moves as well.*
>
> *All sorts of things occur to help one that would never otherwise have occurred. A stream of events issues from the decision, raising in one's favor all manner of unforeseen accidents, meetings, and material assistance which no one could have dreamed would come their way. Whatever you can do or dream you can do, begin it. Boldness has genius, power and magic in it. Begin it now.*
>
> *Johann Wolfgang von Goethe*

Your greatest need right now is the passion for your dream, coupled with a deep desire to make it happen. You took the first step by either purchasing or receiving this book as a gift and reading it to this point.

Whatever you can do or dream you can do, begin it. Boldness has genius, power and magic in it. *Begin it now.*

Remember, only 3% will take the time to write down their dreams, set goals, and take steps to accomplish them. Some qualified analysts set this figure at only 2%.

What happens when you have the added burden of dealing with a major crisis in addition to the ordinary things of life? My prayer is that you find the answer to that question in these pages.

For years I shared with numerous people that in spite of illness, it is necessary to focus on the very thing they find so hard to do—to think about living. They need to dream, plan, write their thoughts, and do what this short book advocates.

Re-read the Goethe quote above. If you focus on the reasons not to begin, you won't. When you get started, no matter how small the effort, you release God's power on your behalf. God intends us to soar like eagles! If we live for His glory, He will make things happen to bring our dreams into reality.

Next, if you have not done so, share with your spouse and most trusted friends what you plan to accomplish. You will discover that ideas come to you so fast that unless you write them down, you will lose most of them.

"You are committed to what you confess." Edwin Louis Cole

I met Edwin Louis Cole while working for the Christian Broadcasting Network. Edwin said, "You are committed to what you confess." It can't be much clearer. As you start talking, you realize you are out there, virtually walking on water. This reality can be frightening but also invigorating. The simplest way is to share your heart with the people who love and believe in you. The ideas will flow.

One other thing Ed Cole said when he challenging men about their lives was, "Write it on your shorts!" Now write your idea in 25 words or less on a 3 x 5 card and do something to keep it in front of you every day for the rest of your life.

Let's Get Going—Start Talking About It!

What's Your Next Step? Finding Mentors

Once you start talking, you need to find a mentor. In my life, I have been fortunate to stumble onto some of the finest mentors anywhere. You need to know who they are and how I found them. Why? Because unless you want to spend time reinventing the wheel, you can save precious time by finding someone who has been down the road and is willing to help you find your way without lost time and effort.

The full-length video, "The Life Giver Story" found on our website, www.tlgn.org, tells the story. Nearly 20 years ago, God called me to change directions and *do something about the cancer issue* affecting so many in a negative way. After the call, I talked to friends about my burden. It took ten months, but after many meetings and much prayer, an action plan unfolded. The result is the James Henry Counseling Associates, which birthed The Life Givers Network. A forthcoming book will present the detailed history and information, and show you how to bring Life Givers to your community.

As I researched ways to help Paula deal with breast cancer, I read *Cancer as a Turning Point,* by Lawrence

LeShan. Deeply moved by Dr. LeShan's work, I decided to do something I had never done. I wanted to meet personally with Dr. LeShan, so I wrote to him through his book agent. Several weeks later, my phone rang, and the voice said, "Hello, this is Larry." This simple request began a lifelong association. Our relationship moved me from uncertainty to knowing I could make a difference.

That year was 1992. Larry had been doing his work since 1947 (I was only two years old!). He was a world leader in helping cancer patients, and all I wanted was to pick his brain. Little did I realize this relationship would move me from uncertainty about my potential to knowing I could make a difference in peoples' lives. By starting to act, and following my heart, God directed me to one of the most knowledgeable authorities about how to help cancer patients.

My Next Two Mentors

After years of helping people, and experiencing cancer 15 times in my family, another of those "miraculous encounters" took my life to a higher level. At 5:00 one morning, I heard a TV infomercial that changed my life. I didn't pay much attention to the man speaking. Then I heard a voice I knew. I looked up to see Gary Smalley endorsing Steven Scott and his "Master Strategies of Super Achievers." Having been to one of Gary's seminars, I knew there had to be some reason for a key Christian leader to endorse someone on TV. I decided to purchase Steven's DVD series. Steven Scott has been highly successful in business, but even more impressive is his devotion to the Lord. Steven attributes his wisdom and success to God. From that moment, Steven Scott became one of my mentors through his DVD's and workbooks. I've watched his DVDs countless times and often listened to his CDs in my car. Steven started more successful companies than anyone I know, and he is humble enough to talk about his failures.

The most important thing I've learned from this experience is that one-tenth of one percent of people who set goals and make plans to achieve them ever become Super Achievers. These are people Steven Scott said would *"shoot for the moon"* when planning and work outside the box.

What did this mean for me? A dreamer like me, whose goal is to see Life Givers in every community in America, now had a mentor who encouraged and helped him do that and not call me crazy.

Our objective is to set high goals, to share with the world what can radically transform lives. Why would we want to do less?

If you have an out-of-this-world dream and want to influence significant numbers of people, get Steve's series.

The Next Step

Because of Steve's series, I spent hours seeking partners to help me live my dream. He says you can get so far on your abilities. But, to reach the moon, you need co-workers to help you in your weak areas, whether business, marketing, or whatever.

As I sought the right mix, an invitation came one day from Dan Miller, speaker, coach, and author of *48 Days to the Work You Love*. The invitation was to a tele-seminar on May 29, 2008, which proved to be another life-changing event.

The afternoon of the teleseminar, my car broke down. It appeared to be a major problem requiring too many dollars, and I didn't have funds for a new car. That

evening I needed someone to pick me up when the
seminar was over and take me home. I began the seminar
very discouraged but was in for the surprise of my life.

That evening, Dan
spoke about the "90
Day Fast Track" pro-
gram to build a new
life. The words kept
going through my
mind: "You can do this." Even though I was not sure
what "this" was, I felt hope rise and determined to
discover what "this" meant for my life.

> **The words kept going through my mind: "You can do this. You have all you need to get your message out."**

That night at home, I realized I was in a situation
similar to many I counseled through the years. Finances
were hard, my car might be down a while, and I wasn't
sure where to turn. Then, the voice of God deep within
me said, "You have all you need to get your message out."

The next two hours, I sat on my sofa with a yellow
legal pad, no TV, no music, no radio, and asked God
what He wanted me to do. He assured me about the
accumulated wealth of experience and information I'd
collected. Much of this information was loaded on the
laptop a good friend gave to our ministry. With my
computer, cell phone, internet, friends, and years of
experience, I had everything needed to reach the world.

The next morning I made a call and was the 25th
person to join *The 212 Connection,* Dan's social network
for entrepreneurs. It was a thrill to be in on the ground
level of this new effort, and I began meeting people,
listening to calls, and gaining new insights every day.
The best part was meeting Dan's son Kevin, founder
of *Free Agent Academy,* and his friend, Chuck Bowen.
These three men led the seminar, and are mentors and
encouragers as I move into new areas. You can be sure
none of this would be happening without these mentors.

Not many would try such an outrageous adventure at age 65, but I'm having the time of my life, knowing we have the potential to impact people all over the world. I'm not beginning my retirement—I'm beginning the second half of my life, which could exceed the first.

If Colonel Sanders could start cooking chicken at 65, I could begin a new life at 65 also. You can too, whatever your age!

If Colonel Sanders could start cooking chicken at 65, I could begin a new life at 65 also, and expect great things to come into and through my life, *You can too, whatever your age!*

Write Your Plan—Work Your Plan

Certainly, over the past few years, my plans to achieve my objective have changed, but my purpose remains the same. My goal has been to establish Life Givers in every community in America. The seminars and the release of this book are significant steps in the direction of fulfilling that dream.

I would be lost without written goals and the plans to achieve them.

With these resources, you have sufficient material to change the rest of your life. I took one thought from Dr. LeShan's books about the importance of why we are created. I continue to work to make that idea come true for others.

Write your plan. Work your plan.

The key is to be flexible. Write your plan. Work your plan. Don't be afraid to fail. Learn from your failures. When something doesn't work, try again. I've had plenty of opportunities to quit. But every time I encourage someone facing an impossible situation, I find I have renewed energy to continue serving, which brings me to my next point.

Keep The Fire Burning

In his thought-provoking book *Holy Discontent*, Pastor Bill Hybels shares what he discovered that keeps the fire burning to fulfill your vision.

His closing chapter is entitled "It Doesn't Have to End Like This." These are the words I use to help so many over the past 27 years. Often I tell patients, "It doesn't have to be that way. We can transform your journey and change the outcome."

> Often I tell patients, "It doesn't have to be that way. We can transform your journey and change the outcome."

When God called me to this work, I was open because of a "Holy Discontent" with how cancer patients and their families were treated after diagnosis. As the old comic hero, Popeye the Sailor Man would say, *"I can't stands no more."* When I couldn't stand what I saw happening anymore, God said, "Do something." So here we are. It's the discontent that insists something has to be different. We must help people "transform the journey and see different outcomes."

It is what we are about. What keeps my fire burning? It's continuing to engage individuals who are in serious crises and helping them find a better way to live. It's replacing the idea that somehow we'll get through to focusing on the future.

> When I couldn't stand what I saw happening anymore, God said, "Do something."

I'm not into coping. I'm into helping people *live*! No matter how bad the prognosis may be.

Keep A Journal

Most people, especially men, find it hard to keep journals. But doing so is essential to fuel your fire. I've kept one for years. No, I'm not always consistent, but I do manage to record the important things. For me, it's more important than ever.

With a written record of your progress, you have reasons to be thankful. That's it. It's not what God is doing in someone else's life but in yours. Nothing can fuel a grateful spirit more than remembering how God helps you.

Whenever I speak, there's nothing people enjoy more than stories. It may have something to do with our mobile society that takes little time to listen and cultivate relationships. But, the best way to make a point is still by telling a story. Your journals record the stories you can draw from to encourage others.

So don't wait. Get a spiral notebook like kids use in school and start keeping notes. Keep them simple. They are your notes. Start now, which tells God you want things to happen and watch what He does.

Develop An Attitude Of Gratitude

As you write, be sure to end each day with thanks to God. Thank Him for open doors and His favor. If you believe that "*Every* good and perfect gift comes from above," thankfulness comes easily at the end of the day.

Late yesterday, while getting ready to head home, I realized how wonderful the day had been. After nearly seven hours writing, I felt energized, not tired. But then something else happened, which resulted in a deep feeling of satisfaction.

Jesus told His disciples, "I have a kind of food you know nothing about." (John 4:32, NLT) What a thrill to find satisfaction and fullness that doesn't come from eating a full meal, but comes from the assurance of doing the will of God. You can have this, too! Seek God first and ask Him to lead you on the path He designed for you. You will have more than enough to be grateful for every day of your life.

One Last Thing — Be Expectant

The Psalmist wrote, "I would have fainted unless I believed the goodness of the Lord in the land of the living." (Psalm 27:13) Me too!

Scott Peck said it best in the opening line of his classic work, *The Road Less Traveled*, "Life is difficult." How true! And things are not getting easier. As life becomes more complex, the problems we have individually and as a country are more challenging. But God does not change. "He is the same, yesterday, today, and forever." (Hebrews 13:8)

Believe God wants good for you. "He takes pleasure in the prosperity of His servants." (Psalm 35:27, AMP) I cling to that promise and encourage you to as well.

Expect God to work on your behalf, to open doors you cannot open, and answer impossible prayers. God's Word says this is what He does for you and me.

> The Psalmist wrote, "I would have fainted unless I believed the goodness of the Lord in the land of the living." (Psalm 27:13)

What Remains?

Nothing, but to get going!

Become Aware

Ask yourself what you are doing about each of the headlines in this chapter.

- Are you committed to your action plan?

- What kind of mentors do you need?

- Who could fill those positions?

- Do you have access to those you need or do you need an introduction?

- Have you written the details of your plan?

- What are you doing to keep the fire of your dream burning?

- Are you truly thankful?

- Are you keeping a journal?

Make card #8

Write: "I will act on my highest priority by (describe first step here)."

Now, take the time to write at least one page, longhand, about your thoughts and feelings after reading this chapter. If you feel led to write more than one page, do so while the ideas are fresh in your mind.

CHAPTER EIGHT
OUTCOMES

One of our primary objectives in Life Givers is "to transform the journey and change the outcomes." When people hear a bad diagnosis, they immediately imagine what the journey will look like. Remember, in Chapter One, I stated we change our focus from the diagnosis is the beginning of the end to it is a new beginning to celebrate *life*.

How Can I Be So Bold About Outcomes?

First, we founded Life Givers based on my calling by God "to do something about this cancer thing" based on Numbers 16:46-48. This call is the result of my life experiences and my discontent while watching people suffer over the first 19 years of my ministry. So, whatever happens, is His doing. All He asked me to do was to get involved, and He would do the work.

Second, being mentored by one of the finest therapists and researchers in the world, I changed my focus from "Can I make a difference?" to the confidence that God would be with me. Seven years later, I realized God had blessed me with confidence that wherever He sent me, no matter how difficult, He would fulfill my desire to see things change.

What allows me to be so bold? First, Life Givers was founded on my calling by God.

Third, God allows me to share with people who are open to this message. These ordinary people see extraordinary things happen in and through them.

Finally, God desires to show His Glory on this earth, and it is His responsibility. I can't make *anything* happen. But knowing His will, and that He is at work on the earth, all pressure is off. I expect Him to be involved unless those who need Him ignore or chase Him away. More about God's glory later.

Confidence Produces Peace

Because of my confidence in the research and what God wanted me to do, I have seen God's peace invade my first face-to-face meetings with people. While I have many examples of this, one of them is especially memorable.

A woman came to see me who had just been diagnosed with very serious cancer. Also, she had family issues that made her poor prognosis even more difficult. Our first conversation lasted about 90 minutes. An hour into the visit, she moved from the edge of the sofa, sat back, and relaxed with a puzzled look on her face. I asked what was wrong. She responded, "I don't know what is happening. I feel so peaceful, more than in a long time." This sensation was the literal peace of God. Each time we met, His peace was palpable. Things kept improving, and she has consistently exceeded her doctor's expectations.

The peace that passes all understanding, described in Philippians 4:6-7, is evident in many other cases. This peace is one of God's promises to those who look to Him for strength and help. Why would any intelligent person say no to His offer of perfect peace even in hard times? Yet some will say no to this offer. Don't be one of these people. You can have this peace. Don't wait. Look to God, and He will give you His peace, which passes all understanding.

> **Why would any intelligent person say no to His offer of perfect peace even in hard times?**

Boldness

Another outcome of following God's path is a *new boldness*. Some develop boldness by listening to stories and insights I share. In Philippians 1:14, Paul tells us *that the brothers, emboldened by his chains, had become more confident and able to share the Word without fear.* When people see others endure extreme circumstances with peace, not fearful or rattled, they wonder how this is possible. The result is developing a win/win attitude and living in a way that generates confidence in others.

> **Another outcome of following God's path is a new boldness.**

Carol, a dear friend who fought cancer for 27 years, came out of her shell about three years before her passing. She attended church and served for many years, but something radically changed her. As she entered a difficult treatment time, I told her our relationship needed to change. After many years of battling, she had much to share and needed to do so. Reluctant, for three weeks, we had serious dialogues about adding this new dimension to her life, but she didn't budge. Then, one day, she said, "Okay, I'll make some of those calls." The next week when she came through my door, she looked at me and began to cry. "I've got to talk with you," she said. Then she told me how blessed she was through those calls. All she needed was to permit herself to get involved. God blessed her and those she spoke with beyond her wildest dreams!

Healing

Everyone wants healing. Even those who believe miracles don't happen anymore, pray God intervenes when a loved one is sick. That is a sign that although they are afraid to believe, and possibly fail, they want to see the miracle.

God wants to dwell among His people. He is all-powerful and all-wise in working His will in the world. My call to this work resulted from a question asked in a graduate school class. We were discussing healing and examining the many different kinds of healing when our professor ended the session with these words: "I want you to think about this question tonight. What are you doing to take healing to people intentionally?" That led me on a three-hour journey with God. Through my search of the Scriptures, He impressed on me those words: ". . . do something about this cancer thing."

> **Even those who believe miracles don't happen anymore, pray God intervenes when a loved one is sick.**

When I asked what He wanted me to do, He was silent. That word in 1991 set me on a course that became my life calling.

Because of this call, and my decision to follow, God allows me to witness every kind of healing. I've seen people experience spiritual healing, moving from death to life. I've watched people who have carried scars for many years healed emotionally. There have been relational healings, physical healings, and divine intervention when expecting disaster.

All because God issued a call, and He wants to show Himself in this world. It's that simple. If we are intentional and believe Him and His Word, He shows us His way. I don't know how He will lead you, but I know He will. And you will know with certainty that it is God at work.

Our Children

One of the profound ways this process impacts people is a positive influence on their children. When a serious illness comes, everything changes. Life is never the same. One of our most important choices, then, is to be better, not bitter. How we live our experience before our children profoundly impacts them for the rest of their lives.

It's easy to bypass this simple point. Your decision to *pursue life*, when it seems impossible, will free your kids from anxiety, spare them from deep grief, and give them memories of life instead of pain and death. Here is an example which I'll always remember.

> *In the mid-nineties, I worked with a woman with severe lung cancer. Although blessed with four children, her life was difficult. She experienced severe*

trauma, which, combined with things at home, made it hard to deal with her cancer. Amid her pain, she gained a new perspective, and made some bold choices. Her expected six-month journey became 18 months. During the last months, she experienced beautiful life moments. When she passed, I spoke with one of her daughters. There, in the funeral home, facing her grief, she told me in great detail how wonderful the last few months of her mom's life had been. She closed with these words: "If it had not been for these past few months, mom's death would have been a tragedy. These months have changed it all and made it so special. Thank you so much."

Let me relate one more thing about our kids. While watching decisions made by friends' children, I've experienced first-hand the choices made by my own. How blessed I am as they choose life. They

Your decision to *pursue life* will free your kids from anxiety, spare them from deep grief, and give them memories of life instead of pain and death.

comment about the good they learned, and make decisions to avoid pain and mistakes. Make your choice.

Leave your kids a legacy, or leave them with baggage. I desire to help you leave a legacy.

Release

In our video series, "Seeds of Light," released in 1999, our main point is God wants to release us into our destiny. We generally call this the will of God for our lives. Dr. LeShan saw one miracle after another when he helped people discover "the song they were created to sing." I've watched so many people come alive when they get "in touch" with why they are here.

About two years after Paula's breast cancer diagnosis, she got in touch with her reason for being. While battling her cancer, she taught children the blessing of music. Two and a half years later, she had taught 1200 students in a school program, plus 40 private students. Some of these appeared in the video. They were her legacy, along with her profound impact on our children.

These brief years were some of Paula's best. She would say, "the very best." I have fond memories of those years. When I think about her, I reflect on the joy we experienced and the energy she received by giving herself to her students.

Think about this. Jesus was on this earth for 33 years; 30 of those years were preparation. He spent three years fulfilling His primary mission of living, dying, and rising again for our salvation.

Life is more than quantity. Many people in their 80s or 90s never come close to accomplishing what Paula and many others do in a brief time. Life is knowing and doing the will of God, fulfilling His purpose with all your heart and soul and strength.

Determine in God's strength to leave a legacy of hope, not grief.

Make this choice now if you have not done so already. Determine in God's strength to leave a legacy of hope, not grief.

The Glory Of God

It is my deep conviction that the most important thing is seeing God's Glory released on the earth.

Many people live in apparently hopeless situations. They wonder about leadership in every area of life, the direction we are headed, the financial chaos, world crises, and so much more. Having to also do battle with a serious illness is almost more than one can bear. God's Word assures us: "God has chosen the foolish things of the world to put to shame the wise, and God has chosen the weak things of the world to put to shame the things that are mighty." (1 Corinthians 1:27) I'm thankful for every caring doctor and what medicine does to help my family. But, medicine falls short, and doctors are forced to say, "I'm sorry, there is nothing more I can do."

I desire that Life Givers reach those caught in these impossible situations. We pray and encourage, then see God intervene and bring glory to Himself. Man fails in every aspect of life. Though our society is ravaged in so many ways, I believe the solution is simple. When we seek God first, and desire to live for His glory, *He will intervene in unexpected ways. He brings a new desire to know and do His will, which ultimately leads us to victory.*

In the summer of 1977, I spent two months with missionaries in Malang, East Java, Indonesia. Malang, a city of some 500,000, had no hospital. To get to the nearest hospital meant an exhausting hour-long trek. Therefore, people either looked to God or witches for help. During my stay in Malang, I saw God work incredible miracles for both nationals and our missionaries. I heard stories about villages turning to God because one person received a miraculous touch from "the Almighty One."

In the villages of Indonesia, I witnessed unexplainable phenomena like those described in the Gospels and the Book of Acts. Jesus, and then His disciples, went everywhere preaching the Gospel and healing the sick. People heard the Good News, and many were saved and healed by the power of God.

Disease is the great equalizer. It impacts young and old, rich and poor, in the city or the country. For the past 27 years, I know whatever help I offer needs to work for any person in any place.

I challenge you to believe and expect with me that all who read this will hunger not only for healing but also for a demonstration of God's power that will impact whole families and entire communities.

> I believe we are lighting a flame. It will cause men and women to seek His help humbly, and ask Him to take control of their lives and their land.

I believe we are lighting a flame that will spread across this nation. This flame will draw attention to God, not to man. It will cause men and women to seek His help humbly, and ask Him to take control of their lives and their land.

Become Aware

For your consideration:

- What are you expecting?

- What are you doing to seek God and the peace He offers?

- What are you doing to take "healing" of all kinds to those in darkness and pain?

- What legacy will you leave for your children?

- What are you doing to discover your calling in life?

- What steps are you taking to let God show Himself through your life?

- Are you willing to proclaim His Glory?

- How might you bring the Good News of His great love to your community, especially to those you love?

Make card #9

Write: "I expect _____ to happen (be specific about what you expect.)"

Now, take the time to write at least one page, longhand, about your thoughts and feelings after reading this chapter. If you feel led to write more than one page, do so while the ideas are fresh in your mind.

CHAPTER NINE
WHAT'S NEXT?

Now that you've completed the first nine cards, it's time to make card #10, your final one.
Write:

> *"I choose to believe I can be a Life Giver and commit to be an active participant in my community."*

Great. It's time to look at the next steps in your journey.

Step #1:

Take a few minutes to note your thoughts and feeling about where you are. You can do this in your journal, on your computer, or an online journal source. It is essential to understand your current mental, emotional, spiritual, relational, and physical states. Often, we don't

take time to reflect and establish a baseline from which
we celebrate our growth. So, let's do that now.

Answer these questions:

- Do you believe the statement about being a Life
  Giver? Do you desire to become one?

- Who were you before reading this book?

- What were your thoughts about your diagnosis or
  that of your loved one?

- What are your thoughts about your future options?

- Who are you right now?

- What transformation do you see?

- How does your future look?

Describe your transformation as thoroughly as you can.

After completing this exercise, you may not be as far along as you desire. That's okay. Celebrate your personal growth up until now.

Alternatively, you may be way ahead of where you thought. Congratulations!

I'm really interested and committed to helping you move toward an abundant and extraordinary life no matter what you may be dealing with or how poor your prognosis might be. The more we understand about your situation, the more we can provide helpful resources.

Now, because my goal is to see lives transformed, send me an email with your answers today. One of the characteristics of successful people is decisiveness. Acting today helps you cultivate that quality in your life. Plus, sending your answers allows me to cheer you on, pray for you, and encourage you.

Send your email to life@tlgn.org. I promise I'll respond to you.

Step #2

Register to receive our email updates. Go to tlgn.org where you can securely enter your online contact information and select exactly the information that helps you the most.

Because we hate spam as much as you do, we do not share your information with anyone. Plus, you can unsubscribe from any or all content at your convenience.

Step #3

Access informational content 24/7/365 on our website.

- Check out our blogs for content that helps you today.
- Watch video posts on the home page of our website (www.tlgn.org).

Step #4

Join our online community. You can find us on Facebook (The Life Givers Network) and LinkedIn (Jim Henry, D. Min)

We consistently post videos as well as written content to encourage you in your life giver journey. Whether you are the one with the life-altering diagnosis, a caregiver, family member, friend, pastor, support person, or someone who wants to help, join our community.

Step #5

Become a member of Life Givers Tribe. Membership has its privileges. Receive twice monthly personal coaching from me. Members only content. Q & A sessions. Plus, you can join our private, members-only Facebook group, an active, vibrant group whose goal is to encourage, provide hope, and generate resources for all members. As people in very difficult places, we believe God can intervene and do extraordinary things in each life, which glorify Him. Cost: $49 per month

Step #6

As a Life Giver, take advantage of our training groups: 4 Essentials, Choices, Going Deeper, and others. Some of these are online trainings, but others are live. And coming shortly will be our members site allowing more personal interaction.

The up-to-date information is in our app, on our website, and our Facebook page. We also email information to anyone who's requested email updates.

Step #7

You've read the content and walked through each healing step. Are you ready to help us spread this life-giving message? If so, enroll in our certification program. Once you complete it, you can open a Life Giver Network site in your area of the world.

Our goal is to reach every country of the world with the Life Giver message. If you want additional information, go to our website (tlgn.org) and send us a message through the contact page.

Step #8

You can help us spread the word by giving back, or as some say, paying it forward. As a non-profit organization, we need supporters who believe in our mission to provide each person we engage with the opportunity to know and experience LIFE to the fullest, Abundant Life according to John 10:10, no matter how severe their diagnosis or how poor their prognosis may be.

We never turn any request for help away. Your prayer and financial support allow us to continue to serve others.

It's simple. Go to tlgn.org and click the donate button. Safe, secure, and life-changing. Thank you.

Final Thoughts

Each year, millions of people receive diagnoses of some kind of major illness. Millions more find themselves in some kind of crisis. Some folks say they don't need God. Others say, "I'm okay. I don't need any help (meaning the human kind)."

Twenty-eight years of this work on a clinical level and over 48 years of ministry have shown me we definitely need both God and each other (see 1 Corinthians 12:20,21).

Joining together for a common objective shows that God can and will make a difference if we let Him. You have nothing to lose and everything, mostly *life*, to gain.

Ultimately, you join others from throughout the United States and abroad, to pray for one another and believe for God's marvelous intervention. Every testimony we receive and share with you through our app, website, and social media networks encourages others in like situations to reach out for help. All we do is for God's glory alone.

My Prayer For Us All:

Father God, I pray for those who are finishing this book and reading this prayer. Impart faith to them and enable them to act as indicated above. Plant in each one a desire to see your glory and power displayed on this earth, and an expectancy that you, Father, will work on their behalf as well as on the behalf of those they love and care for. Help us all to realize the truth of your Word that says, "I would have lost heart, or grown weary, unless I had believed I would see the goodness of God in the land of the living." (Psalm27:13)

AUTHOR'S AFTERWORD
MOUNTAINS

Usually seen as things to be conquered.
Rarely seen as the best vantage point.

For over two decades, I've engaged with people who face impossible challenges—mountains of physical, emotional, and spiritual pain. My objective is to reach the top of this mountain, take a good look, and then help you see the potential for your future.

Some 30 years ago, I heard a message by Judson Cornwall, a gifted minister and Bible teacher from the West Coast. At Blue Mountain Christian Retreat in New Ringgold, Pennsylvania, Cornwall preached an incredible series on Joshua chapter one. His key points was, "When you are on the mountaintop, take a good look around, so when you are in the valley, you will know where to walk."

This story came to my mind recently when God impressed upon me, "Go to the mountain." I knew this voice and was confident He would reveal something special if I listened. Two days later, I drove to the highest point accessible by car in Rocky Mountain National Park. God had something amazing in store!

Driving up Trail Ridge Road is breathtaking. I've never seen anything quite like this spectacular park, with 70 peaks over 12,000 feet above sea level. Entering the park from Estes Park at 7,900 feet, you take Trail Ridge Road 25 miles to the Alpine Visitor's Center at 11,796 feet after passing the highest peak at 12,123. Overwhelmed by the majestic scenery, you see the mountains, lakes, snow, and an occasional Bighorn sheep.

At the Visitor's Center, I saw incredible photos of life on the mountain. A long mural displayed the months of the year and the different animals living on this mountain, almost two miles above sea level. One section caught my attention, which turned on the lights in my heart and mind. The heading and subheading, "Surviving Winter: Tolerate, Migrate, and Hibernate," were like voices booming at me from heaven!

When I saw the words "surviving winter," I knew God was showing me a gateway for persons in crisis.

My map called the entrance to this park, The Gateway to the West. When I saw the words "surviving winter," I knew God was showing me a gateway for persons in crisis, challenged by a *life-threatening situation*. People experience winter when their lives are seriously threatened. The choices to *migrate or hibernate* were clear enough, but what did they mean by *tolerate?* Their definition was not what I expected. It was not about *coping*. It was *to remain active and adapt*. Wow! I saw it!

The Parks Department's prime example is a small bird known as a *ptarmigan*. It tolerates the long, bitter winters. Molting several times a year, it changes color with the season—brown in the summer and white in the winter. But far more significant, *in winter, it is covered with insulating feathers. God describes how He does the same for us in Psalm 91:4, where He speaks of being hidden under His wings.*

Here, two miles above sea level, God used the park's informative article to show me how survival in the worst of conditions is possible. *Remain active, adapt, and cover yourself* with insulating feathers.

It is our Life Givers message—hope and life to people, no matter how bad their situation. It is the message of this book—the impossible can be possible. Experience extraordinary life in the face of death.

What an incredible lesson! Here at the "Gateway to the West," God affirmed it is possible to survive the very worst. This was it! By going to the top of the mountain, in obedience to seek God's instruction, I found *the Gateway!*

This book is your gateway! Instead of seeing your challenge as a mountain to be removed, accept it as God's opportunity to take you to the peak, to show you what you have never seen before.

As Judson Cornwall said, instead of trying to remove the mountain, while you're up there, take a look around so you will know how to walk when you're back in the valley where you spend most of your

> Instead of seeing your challenge as a mountain to be removed, accept it as God's opportunity to take you to the peak, to show you what you have never seen before.

years. Amazingly, when you focus on living instead of moving mountains, the mountains begin to disappear.

Thank you for taking this journey with me. If you need help, please contact me. Remember, your life, no matter the length can be better than ever before when you put your trust and hope in God.

> **Remember, your life, no matter the length can be better than ever before when you put your trust and hope in God.**

Let me leave you with the following two verses, which are a source of great hope and encouragement for me:

"I would have lost heart unless I believed that I would see the goodness of the Lord in the land of the living." Psalm 27:13 NKJV

"And I am convinced and sure of this very thing, that He Who began a good work in you will continue until the day of Jesus Christ (right up to the time of His return), developing (that good work) and perfecting and bringing it to full completion in you." Philippians 1:6 AMP

Jim Henry
October 2011

SUGGESTED READING

A few key books for those who want to fight for their lives:

The Bible

Recommended versions include the New King James Version (NKJV), the New International Version (NIV), the New American Standard Version (NASV), and the Amplified version (AMP).

Modern translations some may want to consider include the Living Bible (LB), the New Living Translation (NLT), and The Message. The recommended versions are generally considered more accurate in their translation of the original texts.

Batterson, Mark, *In a Pit With a Lion on a Snowy Day*,
Multnomah Books, ISBN 978-1-60142-364-1

Carpenter, Ron Jr., *The Necessity of An Enemy*,
Waterbrook Press, ISBN 978-0-307-73028-2

Conwell, Russell, *Acres of Diamonds*,
available on Kindle for free

Cornwall, Judson, *Dying with Grace*,
Charisma House, ISBN 1-59185-453-9

Cousins, Norman, *Anatomy of an Illness*,
Bantam Books, ISBN 0-553-34365-3

Elliot, Elizabeth, *A Path Through Suffering*,
Servant Publications, ISBN 0-89283-801-9

Hayford, Jack, *Hope for a Hopeless Day*,
Regal Books, ISBN 0-8307-4494-0

Hutschnecker, Arnold, *The Will to Live*,
Simon & Schuster, ISBN 0-346-12555-3

Keller, Phillip, *A Shepherd Looks at the 23rd Psalm*,
Zondervan Publishing House, ISBN 0-310-26790-0

Kendall, R.T., *Believing God,*
Morning Star Publications & Ministries,
ISBN 1-878327-63-1

Kendall, R.T., *Total Forgiveness,*
Charisma House, ISBN 0-88419-889-8

LeShan, Lawrence, *Cancer As A Turning Point,*
Plume/Penguin, ISBN 0-8362-2415-9

LeShan, Lawrence, *You Can Fight for Your Life,*
M. Evens & Co., ISBN 0-87131-494-0

Mehl, Ron, *A Prayer that Moves Heaven,*
Multnomah Books, ISBN 1-59051-890-5

Murray, Andrew, *With Christ in the School of Prayer,*
Spire Books, ISBN 1-42096-106-3

Sheets, Dutch, *Hope Resurrected,*
Regal Books, ISBN 0-8307-3624-7

Siegel, Bernie, Love, *Medicine, and Miracles,*
Harper & Row, ISBN 0-06-091-406-8

Simonton, Carl O., *Getting Well Again,*
Bantam Books, ISBN 0-8054-9994-7

Smith, Hyrum W., *What Matters Most,*
Fireside Books, ISBN 0-684-87257-9

Spiegel, David, *Living Beyond Limits,*
Fawcett Columbine, ISBN 0-8007-5124-8

CONTACT INFORMATION

Dr. Jim Henry, Founder
The Life Givers Network®
PO Box 110
Midland Park, NJ 07432

Email: life@tlgn.org

FOR INTERNET BOOK ORDERS
Go to our secure page at www.tlgn.org

Also available wherever books are sold.

CPSIA information can be obtained
at www.ICGtesting.com
Printed in the USA
LVHW021819160320
650193LV00002B/103